CHOSEN
IN THE
FURNACE

CHOSEN
IN THE
FURNACE

*A Testimony of Survival
and a Guide to All Who
Desire to be Encouragers*

Chris and Jim Robinson

YorkshirePublishing
www.yorkshirepublishing.com
Write Now.

ISBN: 978-1-947491-76-2

Chosen in the Furnace

For permission requests, write to the publisher at the address below.

Yorkshire Publishing
3207 South Norwood Avenue
Tulsa, Oklahoma 74135
www.YorkshirePublishing.com
918.394.2665

Acknowledgments

To my dear husband and friend, I can never thank you enough for standing by me. You have been a good listener, counselor, and encourager. Jim helped me with the writing and editing and added his own comments found in boxes throughout the book.

I also want to thank my precious mother, Ellen McAdams (who went to be with the Lord during the writing of the book), my sister Francine (who made the suggestion to journal my thoughts over the last twenty-five years), and our daughters Kerry and Kristin, to whom I owe so much for their patient love and support.

To all the many other family members and friends who have been there for me with their continued prayers and support, I can't thank you enough.

About the Authors

Jim and Chris began their ministry after Jim's graduation from Southwestern Assemblies of God University in 1969. During his service in the military, they ministered in a church in New Mexico and in air force and army chapel groups in Germany. After Jim's discharge from the military, they served churches in Arkansas, Tennessee, and Texas. Altogether, they have over thirty years of pastoral ministry experience.

During their pastorate in Tennessee, Jim received further undergraduate and graduate education through Middle Tennessee State University. He has taught psychology, child psychology, and marriage and family courses on the college level and written an *Introduction to Pastoral Counseling* textbook used by Global University of the Assemblies of God.

Growing up in a minister's home, Chris became well acquainted with all types of church work. She is proficient in both piano and organ and has been involved in music ministry most of her life. She has also served in their pastorates as a teacher, speaker, and women's group leader.

One of the turning points of their ministry took place in the mid-1980s when Chris was stricken with severe clinical depression. Hospitalized several times, she underwent Electroconvulsive therapy (ECT) on two different occasions before finally taking the long road toward recovery. Since then, she has had opportunity to minister to others who have also struggled with major depression. Together, Jim and Chris have been able to bring both clinical instruction and biblical encouragement to many individuals and families who have been affected by emotional and mental disorders.

Jim and Chris have two daughters—Kerry Beaman, who lives in Springfield, Missouri, with husband Ron and children Devon and Kendall; and Kristin McDonald-Willey, who lives in Amarillo, Texas, with her husband Ryan.

Contents

Introduction

· · · · · · · · · · · · · · · · · ·

Sing, O heavens; and be joyful, O earth; and break
forth into singing, O mountains: for the Lord has
comforted his people, and will have mercy upon
his afflicted.

—Isaiah 49:13 (KJV)

GOD HAS USED many people to offer me the help and
encouragement I so desperately have needed. In the darkest periods of my depression, God has been faithful to send
me special messages of hope from many different sources,
which have become very precious in my memory.

The things that I share here from my personal experience cannot substitute for the individual guidance that
God personalizes for each of His children. However, in
almost every kind of trial, I believe God enlightens certain
principles of truth to us for our sustenance and guidance.

Even when we seemingly have become humanly incapable of finding direction, the Holy Spirit is faithful to lead
us. There will always be those limitations of human knowl-

edge and wisdom that could cripple us and even threaten our very survival. However, I believe God has placed within us the ability to recognize our insufficiencies and offer us the opportunity to find Him.

When we are limited in our resources, we find the One who promised, "I will never leave you nor forsake you" (Heb. 13:5, NKJV). He is a Sustainer, a Deliverer, a Protector, and an Encourager. He meets the most vital needs that we will ever have.

I do not believe I could have survived and come this far without God's help. There may be others who have endured depression without God, but I have found that in turning to Him, I have found so much more than mere endurance. I have found a rewarding journey of contentment and joy that has enabled me to establish meaning to my life and deepen my relationship with the Almighty. Seeking Him has become the greatest thrill that I have experienced in this life, and I have found His promise to be *closer than a brother* a personal reality.

God may use others to bring occasional help and encouragement, but ultimately, we all must be brought to the realization that He is our primary source for wholeness and fulfillment. I have found truth in the scripture, "He satisfies the longing soul, and fills the hungry soul with goodness" (Ps. 107:9, NKJV).

Many of the insights that I now treasure and share here came out of experiences that, at the time, seemed impossible to overcome. I certainly do not claim to have found all the "secrets" of dealing with depression or other significant times of crisis. There are some things that defy our attempts to attach explanations and/or reasons—even after a lifetime. In our search for facts and understanding, we must always, in the end, rely upon an unshakable trust in God and His sovereignty as He works in our lives. All must come to the foundational truth for peaceful living, which is to believe and trust in our Creator. To arrive at any other conclusion is to miss the intended primary purpose of this book.

It may be difficult, at times, to understand how to exercise one's faith, but God will teach all who have a hunger in their hearts to know Him. You may wonder, as I did, whether or not you *have* any faith to exercise. But those who search for Him will find Him, and to them, He will make His truth known.

To anyone trying to fight through his or her struggles without a personal relationship with God, I want to encourage you that He wants you to let him help, and His greatest desire is that you would come to know Him as a personal friend.

Foreword

MY PURPOSE IN writing this book is to pass on what I have learned to others who may be struggling with clinical depression. I have encountered many triumphs, failures, and setbacks with this condition over many years and do not believe there could be anything worse than the physical, mental, and emotional pain that results from its torment and anguish.

Chosen in the Furnace is not just a testimony of my struggle with a medical condition; it is also a story about the internal changes that have occurred within me personally—changes that took place as I faced my own weaknesses through difficult struggles and confrontations during the greatest crisis of my life.

I believe God often uses our trials to produce spiritual fruit that might not otherwise emerge (1 Pet. 4:12–13, 5:10). That is not to say that God *caused* the depression; however, I do believe God has purpose in whatever happens in our lives and can take the bad and turn it around for our good, if we allow Him the opportunity (Gen. 50:20). I do know that in my case, it was through the fiery furnace of affliction that the fruit I had longed for began to appear.

The affliction was not always easy to deal with, nor have I liked the internal struggles it has produced. However, as time has passed, little by little, I have begun to see some of the changes God has made and can say with the psalmist, "It is good for me that I have been afflicted; that I might learn thy statutes" (Ps. 119:71, KJV). When I began to see *purpose* in my affliction, it suddenly began to take on personal meaning that helped me endure.

My understanding of *divine purpose* required a breaking process that began at the very core of my being. During that process, God allowed everything that *could be* shaken to *be* shaken so that only His truth would remain (Heb. 12:27). I found that leaning completely on Christ results in building a sure foundation of faith that enables one to stand whatever storms of life might come. I learned the importance of making the Word of God my first priority, allowing it to illuminate my darkness.

In my years of searching for reasons, God has not always given me all the answers I wanted. However, He has given me sufficient understanding and encouragement so that I can press on.

Perhaps something related here will meet that need in others. I pray that God will use this testimony to provide comfort and encouragement to fellow sufferers of depression. Also, I hope those in a *supportive role* (of people in depression) may find some insights here, which will enable them to be more compassionate and effective in their ministry.

PART I

SEASONS OF CHANGE

Awake, north wind, and come, south wind!
Blow on my garden, that its fragrance may spread abroad.

—Song of Solomon 4:16 (NIV)

1

TO KNOW HIM

I REMEMBER VIVIDLY sitting at the piano and singing, "Whatever it takes to draw closer to you Lord, That's what I'll be willing to do."[1]

I sang with all my heart, the tears running down my cheeks. As Paul wrote so earnestly to the believers in Philippi (Phil. 3:10, NKJV) of his desire to "know him, and the power of his resurrection, and the fellowship of his sufferings," I too wanted to know God and experience a more intimate relationship with Him.

I wondered what it would take for my longing to be filled. I did so want to be more like Jesus, and surely, God wouldn't withhold from me that deep and urgent desire.

My husband and I were in our first pastorate, where after years of service, we were finally experiencing revival and a real move of the Spirit. The church was growing, and we were making plans to relocate to a larger piece of property and build new church facilities. It was only a short time after my expressed yearning at the piano that things began falling apart.

As often happens in any ministry endeavor, Satan began to launch an all-out attack upon everything and everyone around me. One crisis after another began taking place in our family. Satan's tactics haven't really changed that much down through history. It is interesting to note that Satan often comes against those who are the closest to us. Job is a prime example as Satan began by targeting his immediate family (Job 1–2).

In my case, Satan's first target was my sister. After several years of marriage and fruitful ministry as a pastor and foreign missionary, her marriage came to a sudden end. She was forced to depart the land of her calling to fly back to the States and try to put her life back together. Her divorce was devastating to all of us.

It was not long after receiving the news of my sister's divorce that I began experiencing some serious health issues. To begin with, I started experiencing excruciating pain in my lower back. Simply walking across a room became difficult for me. To add to my pain, I began having panic attacks (which, at that time, I was not sure I even knew what they were). My back became so bad that my legs would simply give way if I tried to stand. I thought perhaps I needed bed rest to ease the pain, but whenever I lay down, Satan would torment my mind with endless questions such as:

- Why is my world falling apart?
- Is this the reward God gives to those who are trying to serve Him?
- Why is everything suddenly going so wrong?

Nothing I attempted to do was changing anything!

I had been raised in a minister's home where God had always been at the center of everything. Church, prayer, and nightly devotions were part of my normal routine. God had been a central and integral part of my whole life. Growing up, I had been surrounded by an atmosphere of faith and trust, often punctuated by testimonies of a faithful and wonderful God.

In a way, I had been somewhat insulated from any real-life problems. Now I found myself encountering a part of my spiritual journey that I had not previously experienced. I found myself facing a real Goliath! Naively, I had developed the unrealistic concept that if a person were a Christian committed to God's service, he or she wouldn't have to deal with any real challenges. Up until that time, most of my relationship with God had focused on His promises to help and deliver us from any problems. So as I began my search for quick answers, I was quite surprised to find that things were not always as simplistic as I had thought.

> For He makes his sun rise on the evil and on the good, and sends rain on the just and on the unjust. (Matt. 5:45, ESV)

> I returned and saw under the sun that the race is not to the swift nor the battle to the strong, neither is bread to the wise nor riches to men of intelligence and understanding nor favor to men of skill; but time and chance happen to them all. (Eccles. 9:11, AMP)

To create a solid foundation for our faith, we must take the whole Word of God.

Looking back, I can see that my failure to understand the whole scope of Christian living accurately was perhaps due to the fact that I had never really pushed myself to dig out God's Word for myself on a more personal level. I was a third-generation Christian, and most of what I had learned was through observing great people of faith and gleaning from their testimonies. I had inadvertently fallen into the trap of thinking that my own personal faith could somehow be developed through a spiritual osmosis.

Of course, there had been many times when I had personally experienced God's presence and comfort. I had never, however, had to wage any serious spiritual battles of my own or claim victories through my own personal fight of faith. Previous to this crisis, I had relied upon the prayers and encouragement given me by my parents. Now, for the first time in my life, I was being faced with a situation that was now challenging my faith on a strictly personal level.

I was at a crossroads!

I loved God, but I (like many Christians, I suppose) had never given Christ first place and true lordship of my life. I really didn't know the extent and cost of true discipleship or what it entailed. I prayed and read my Bible occasionally but had never developed any level of consistency. My spiritual life was like a yo-yo—up and then down, depending on my circumstances and moods.

I figured as long as I was staying busy, my work for God would be enough. I had many good priorities—my family and church work—but too often, it was only the leftover time that I gave for building a personal relationship with God. Mine was the all too often case of being wrapped up in ministry for God but too busy for God Himself. I hadn't learned yet that the greatest act of true ministry and worship is the time we spend with God. That is not to say that it is necessarily the amount of time we give that counts; however, it is to state that our relationship with God depends a great deal upon our fellowship with Him, and His deepest desire is to fellowship with His children.

If we are not willing to give Christ the first fruits of our lives, we often end up not even giving him the fragments!

Nothing is more important than developing and maintaining a personal relationship with our blessed Savior. There is no amount of Christian service that will ever bring to us the complete satisfaction that only Christ Himself can bring. We are empty vessels without him. God has created in us a void that can never be filled, except by giving Him first place in our lives. Throughout His Word, God expresses His desire to draw us to Him.

Wasn't that the cry of Jesus as he looked out over Jerusalem? He wept as He said, "How often would I have gathered your children together as a hen gathers her brood under her wings, and you were not willing" (Matt. 23:37 English Standard Version). To the *Laodicean Church*, He calls out not to unbelievers but to His own, as He says, "Behold, I stand at the door and knock. If anyone hears my voice and opens the door, I will come in to him and eat with him, and he with me" (Rev. 3:20, ESV).

I'm sure that all too often, Jesus was left standing at my door because I was just too busy.

Why is it we would never insult another human friend in such a manner, and yet we often bring great hurt to the heart of God when we keep Him at such arm's length? He wants to be our confidante and longs for our fellowship. He bids us to worship Him in spirit as well as in truth—inwardly as well as outwardly.

A personal relationship must be established!

And so, in God's sovereignty, He will sometimes allow us to experience great need, in order to encourage us to draw closer to him. We also find that God's purpose in adversity is often twofold—to strengthen our faith and to make us fruitful. It was crisis that became the catalyst used to magnify God's Word to me and to motivate me to seek Him wholeheartedly.

Paul reiterated this truth when he cried, "Oh, the depth of the riches and wisdom and knowledge of God! (Rom. 11:33, ESV). The more God began showing me His revealed Word, the more I hungered for it. And yet, in spite of all my hunger, the affliction still remained. At the time, it was a great discouragement to me that the affliction wasn't removed; however, as time passed, I began to see that God's tests are often for a season.

"In this you greatly rejoice, though now for a little while, if need be, you have been grieved by various trials" (1 Pet. 1:6).

Faith is more than a gift, more than a feeling, more than a belief or assurance. It is a choice to believe, based on nothing more than God's immutable Word.

When going through hard times, one may wonder (as I did), "Why should I have to go through this?" In my case, I had to learn to let go the reins of my life and accept the fact that God really was in control. He knew full well what was going on in my life, even though I didn't understand why I had to endure the present pain. I discovered that to believe in His sovereignty, I had to choose to believe that He *did* care—whether or not the circumstances seemed to support that truth.

Jeremiah wrote, "For he doth not afflict willingly nor grieve the children of men" (Lam. 3:33, KJV). Many times, He allows us to be seemingly backed up against unmovable walls so that our eyes can be opened to what He is endeavoring to accomplish in our lives.

That is usually the time when He allows a tremendous upheaval of things around us to take place. The writer of Hebrews reminds us that God will allow "the removing of those things that are shaken ... that those things which cannot be shaken may remain" (Heb. 12:27, KJV). When the pieces of our lives look like they are in complete ruin, it is often then that God steps in and begins to bring us toward wholeness and fruitfulness.

Change comes through recognizing our weakness.

God reveals to us our weakness so that we might desire change. In the book *Broken Bread*, author John Follette points out that the word *tribulation* actually means *threshing*.[2] As a farmer threshes the golden wheat to separate the chaff and the sticks, so it is in our lives.

Our trials will either break us in spirit, melting the hardness and bringing us in our helplessness to God, or as Follette writes, it will make us "bitter or resentful, or...hard, cruel, and cynical."[3] In essence, it will either make us bitter or better. God's ultimate design for trouble is to teach us that we can learn to use it as our servant, in order that we might become more and more like Christ.

Follette illustrates that principle with the following poem:

Trouble Is a Servant

All of us know trouble—at least I hope we do;
Trouble is a servant, but known as such to few.
We are taught to shun her and, if she comes too near,
Seldom do we face her but run away in fear.
Good and bad must meet her, the universe around—
Sinners, saints, kings and knaves—she comes where
    man is found.
Always make her serve you, for she can serve you
    well;
Just HOW you may use her—your life will always
    tell.
Trouble is but passive—it's by our power to will—
We make her either bless us or do the soul some ill.
How do you translate her from phrases filled with
    pain
To messages of strength—from loss to endless gain?
By faith we see behind the outer frightful mask—
A servant in disguise, to do a gracious task.
Hearts may feel her wounding and life may suffer loss;
Faith translates her working, as freeing gold from
    dross.
Trouble will discover to any yielded heart
Hidden depths of power it only knew in part;
Sympathizing power, and love that understands;

Strength to help another with trouble-tested hands.
Trouble will release you from self and make you kind,
Adding new dimensions to heart and soul and mind.
Do not shun this servant, but look beyond her task
To beauty she will work—for which you daily ask.
Always see in trouble a chance to grow in grace,
Not a stroke of evil to hinder in your race.
Live the life triumphant above her fiery darts;
Rich fruitage will be yours to share with needy hearts.[4]

God uses trouble and tribulation to help separate the wheat from the chaff and make our faith into something that is much more precious than gold. I, like most people (tongue in cheek), didn't want the trouble, but I sure wanted the gold! God, however, always faithful to his Word, continued to work with me as He used the tool of trouble to fan my desire.

If we want to know God more, He will give us that opportunity. Deuteronomy 4:29 (ESV) says, "But from there you will seek the Lord your God, and you will find Him, if you search after Him with all your heart and with all your soul." It is a great encouragement to know that it doesn't matter about the past or what we are going through in the present. If we are willing for Him to begin His work, He immediately begins to do whatever it takes to bring it about within us. Though we may feel that we don't have anything for Him to work with, He can still reach inside of us and draw out the previously unknown potential. He can change whatever needs to be changed, even when we may not have been as sensitive or diligent in our search as we should have been.

I felt unworthy because I had failed so many times. God, however, in His grace and mercy, always looked beyond my past history to make each day a new beginning. And one of the greatest truths I discovered was that God already knew me anyhow. "You know my sitting down and my rising up; you understand my thought afar off. You comprehend my path and my lying down, and are acquainted with all my way" (Ps. 139:2, NKJV). Even when He knew the worst about Israel, He said, "For I know the thoughts that I think toward you, says the Lord, thoughts of peace and not of evil, to give you a future and a hope" (Jer. 29:11, NKJV). The same is true about us.

As we begin to seek Him, we will also come to know Him, and getting to know God is the most satisfying journey we will ever find in this life. He offers us salvation from our sin, but that is only the starting point. He goes on to say that He has "given to us all things that pertain to life and godliness" (2 Pet. 1:3, NKJV). If we stop with salvation alone, we will only be partially fulfilled and satisfied with our spiritual lives.

In order to find fulfillment and satisfaction, it is imperative that we have not only a *saving* revelation of Christ but also a *growing* and *dynamic* revelation. That enables us to continue walking with God through the ups and downs of life. The good thing is that God will be there to sustain us as we allow his transforming power to mold us and change us. Philippians 2:13 (NKJV) reminds us, "For it is God who works in you both to will and to do for His good pleasure." Getting to know God and building a strong faith starts with a willing heart and a submission to His master plan.

I received an unexpected and unwelcome diagnosis.

I knew I needed a lot of internal changes, because my inability to cope had finally manifested itself. My great need had brought me to the realization that God must change me if I were going to survive this crisis. For a time, though, things just continued to get worse.

"And a great windstorm arose" (Mark 4:37, NKJV). In addition to receiving the bad news about my sister and suffering the onset of horrific back pains, I began having (what was later diagnosed as) panic attacks. At that point, I decided it might be wise to get a medical opinion. The first doctor I went to bluntly told me I was having a nervous breakdown. I couldn't believe such a thing was possible for a Christian, so I decided to get a second opinion. It was kind of like hunting for different versions of the Bible until I found one that said what I wanted it to say! When the second doctor announced, "Lady, you have clinical depression," I was astounded. Like many others (especially in the church world), I did not even know what clinical depression meant. I knew that sometimes, when one feels down, the person might say he or she is depressed. But *clinical depression* was completely new terminology to me.

What is Clinical Depression?

Clinical (or *major*) *depression* is not the same as the *general* depression that everyone experiences from time to time. Occasionally, most people feel down or have the blues, but it is usually a temporary condition.

Clinical depression is sometimes called the common cold of emotional disorders. Millions of Americans suffer from this kind of depression, and it is estimated that around 12 percent of men and women will have an encounter with major depression at some point in their lives. Although the condition seems to be more prevalent in women than in men, it is not uncommon to find the disorder affecting both genders and all age groups.

The illness has nothing to do with one's character, nor is it a condition that strikes any particular type of person. Abraham Lincoln, Winston Churchill, Charles Spurgeon, Martin Luther, John Bunyan, and Bible translator J. B. Phillips are just representative of thousands of people who have battled the darkness of deep depression.

Though sometimes a cause may be *assumed* for the condition, there may be no *apparent* reason for depression to strike. Clinical depression is a *medical* condition caused by *biological* malfunction, much the same as diabetes, asthma, or any other (physical) illness. Chemical neurotransmitters are involved in the delivery of messages to the brain that control thinking processes and moods. When there is a disruption of those biological processes, an emotional breakdown can result.

I saw my situation from a very limited spiritual perspective, and the whole idea of clinical depression totally confused me. Didn't the scripture say we were to have peace and joy in Christ? Surely then, Christians could never suffer from depression!

Many Christians do not believe that people who love and serve God with all their hearts should ever struggle with mental or emotional disorders. That places a terrible burden upon the sufferers, who are forced to conclude that the condition must be entirely their own fault. In vain, they try to fix the problem all by themselves, ashamed to admit their "weakness" to people or to God.

But God is not waiting for us to get it altogether before He will offer His Help to us! He meets us where we are, regardless of what our situation may be. In Psalms 139:7–8 (NKJV), David said, "Where can I go from your spirit?...If I make my bed in hell, behold, you are there." Even to the person in depression, God can—somehow, someway—make Himself known to the sufferer. However, the realization that God is fully aware of one's hell-like existence may (and often does) take time.

Sometimes, our dependence on others is taken away.

After receiving my second diagnosis, I remember calling my dad. I had always gone to him whenever I was facing any conflict. I just knew he would say something that would make the depression go away. He had always been able to calm my fears by giving me a scripture or word of encouragement. As I anxiously waited for the call to go through, it was my mother who answered the phone. She informed me that Dad had been quite ill and was not able to speak to me. Not understanding the seriousness of his situation, I begged her to let me talk to him. Finally, in spite of his weakness, she helped him to the phone. His voice was so weak I could barely hear him. Still unmindful of *his* difficulty, I began pouring out *my* troubles, telling him how I had just been diagnosed with clinical depression and didn't know what to do.

Very softly, he replied, "Honey, all I can do right now is pray for you because I'm just too weak to talk. As my mother took back the phone, I cried out, "What's wrong with Dad?" She then informed me that he had been suffering from congestive heart failure. My Rock of Gibraltar wasn't able to help me. All my former lifelines were suddenly being cut off. Now it was just God and I.

I cannot adequately describe the terror that gripped me. My world was absolutely falling apart. Here was yet another crisis in my family. Didn't God know I had always leaned on my dad, and now he wasn't there for me? What could I do now? Who was going to help me? It would be some time before I began to realize that God was allowing the people I had leaned on to be temporarily removed, one by one, from my life.

God often uses the urgency of our situation to help us discover the real need in our lives.

In the beginning, I believed that my *healing* was the only important issue. I reasoned that if I could only find the right spiritual formula, my condition would surely change. It was becoming very difficult to deal with the weaknesses that I began to see within myself. I had always thought of myself as a strong, independent person, but the self-image I had erected was being torn apart. I didn't know who I really was. In the midst of my dark experience, I realized for the first time in my life that even the seemingly strong must still recognize the need for leaning upon God! This passage from *Streams in the Desert* says:

> The capacity for knowing God enlarges as we are brought by Him into circumstances which oblige us to exercise faith; so, when difficulties beset our path, let us thank God that He is taking trouble with us and lean hard upon Him.[5]

God was allowing my weakness to be exposed and my need of Him to be fully revealed. I was slowly becoming aware that I needed more than a physical healing. I needed to be changed. I needed a new revelation of God that would create within me a willingness to be fashioned more in His image.

Should Christians Have Clinical Depression?

Many people (especially those from evangelical churches) have heard that Christians should always exhibit the fruit of the Spirit—especially joy and peace. They have also heard a great deal of teaching on the subject of faith, which is often construed as a frame of mind and attitude that is in direct opposition to depression.

Therefore, their first response to the question would be, "Christians should *never* be depressed!"

The problem lies in how one defines the term: if we are speaking of depression simply as a general mood or demeanor, we might all agree that Christians should be positive and Christlike in their everyday lives.

However, if we are speaking of depression as a medical condition, the response might (and should) be different. The question then could just as well be, "Can Christians get (physically) sick?" And while there are some who might declare, "They *shouldn't!*" most would not go to that extreme.

Checking Up

- ✓ The process of knowing Christ is initiated by hunger and desire and is often propelled by a crisis experience.
- ✓ When we move toward God, Satan often launches an all-out personal attack against us and/or people close to us.
- ✓ God's people are not exempt from the pressures of life.
- ✓ We cannot share someone else's relationship with God.
- ✓ We can become involved in ministry for God at the expense of a relationship with God.

✓ Seasons of testing are normal for everyone.
✓ God reveals our weakness so that we might desire change.
✓ God uses tribulations to remove the things in our life that obscure the reflection of Christ.
✓ Building a strong faith starts with a willing heart and a submission to God's plan.
✓ God faithfully meets us where we are!
✓ God may allow some of our support systems to be cut off so that we might be encouraged to seek Him for ourselves.
✓ God often uses a problem to help us discover our real needs.

2

GRASPING AT STRAWS

My soul, wait thou only upon God.

—Psalm 62:5 KJV

AS A CHILD, I had learned that Christ experienced an agony that is still difficult for me to comprehend (Mark 15:33–34). Because Christ was willing to take upon Himself the sins of mankind, He was able to identify with all human weakness and pain (Heb. 4:15). I had been taught the scripture,

> For He himself [in His humanity] has suffered in being tempted (tested and tried), He is able (immediately) to run to the cry of (assist, relieve) those who are being tempted and tested *and* tried [and who therefore are being exposed to suffering]. (Heb. 2:18, AMP)

Yet as the depression deepened, it seemed that God had turned His back on me. I felt no relief, assurance, or comfort. In fact, I could no longer sense His presence at all. It felt as if darkness had closed in and isolated me from every source of comfort. All I could see was the utter hopelessness of my condition. At that time, the notion that God would help me was beyond my ability to grasp or think. I began searching desperately for answers.

Of course, there was no shortage of advice! Everywhere I turned, there was someone with a surefire approach to resolve my dilemma. One would say, "If you'll just try this...," and then someone else would suggest something entirely different. In my confusion, I began grasping at one straw after another. Looking back, I wish I could have realized that God had never left me; He was there to help me through all my conflicts. However, due to the condition itself, it seemed I could neither reason nor exercise proper spiritual discernment.

So Many Counselors!

In the book of Proverbs (chapters 11, 15, 24) there are references about the wisdom of seeking counsel from multiple sources. The context of those verses relates to a king seeking guidance from trusted advisors pertaining to the complex issues of government and politics. In looking to many counselors, the king could discern the best course of action to take in the nation's interest, and, at the same time, protect himself from making rash decisions on his own.

The individual seeking personal spiritual and emotional stability, however, can become even more confused by listening to everyone who wants to give advice. While it is natural to want to try anything and everything in hope of finding escape from depression's darkness, it is much better to follow a consistent course set by a trained, Godly caregiver, and/or a trusted team who is working together and speaking the same thing.

I was in complete denial.

Though my condition had been diagnosed by a competent professional, I continued to search for another, more acceptable opinion. I didn't realize that along with being depressed, the very foundations of my faith were being shaken. I now realize that when our faith is put on trial, there is usually a period of time that must pass before we begin to see any manifestation of God's help and provision.

I am reminded of the verse that tells us,

> For you have need of steadfast patience and endurance, so that you may perform and fully accomplish

the will of God, and thus receive and carry away [and enjoy to the full] what is promised. (Heb. 10:36 AMP)

Referring to Abraham, Romans 4:18 says, "Who against hope believed in hope" (NKJV).

Though his faith was tried for a long period of time, he never stopped hoping.

However, I had not as yet learned many of faith's lessons. I think the most important lesson I had to learn first was "Walking by faith means choosing to trust God and continuing to trust God, even when we don't understand His workings or have a clue of what He's up to!"

When instant relief did not come, I felt that God surely must have turned against me. I realize now that I have not been the only one who has had such tormenting thoughts. That was the great mental anguish that Job experienced when he said that God had made him his target. His words were full of grief as he lamented, "The arrows of the Almighty are within me...the terrors of God do set themselves in array against me" (Job 6:4 AMP).

I did not—and could not—realize at the time that Satan, in an attempt to destroy my faith, wanted to make me believe that God had forsaken me.

Due to the chemical imbalance, it seemed impossible to find any lasting place of peace. Because I refused to accept the diagnosis of depression, I went from one doctor to another to find out what was really wrong. More tests were run, which only proved to be more wasted time and money. I found myself identifying with the woman with the issue of blood who had spent all that she had seeking cures (Luke 8).

My grasping at straws turned into an endless and fruitless search. I desperately wanted my condition to be something other than depression. It was impossible for me to accept that I could be suffering from any kind of an "emotional disorder." I don't think I had ever heard of Christians having emotional problems because in Christian circles, it was never admitted or even talked about.

Still a Stigma!

Because most Christians have accepted sickness as a result of Adam's fall and our having to live in an imperfect world, they tend to be compassionate toward those with physical illnesses and/or injuries. There is no reason to hide those kinds of ailments, and praying for the sick has become normal and acceptable in most Christian circles.

There is, however, still a stigma attached to mental and/or emotional disorders. In the minds of many, those problems are often associated with character flaws, spiritual lack, or unconfessed sin. Consequently, neither the sufferer nor those around him or her wants to address those difficulties.

Now years later, I am beginning to see more of an openness and understanding from the Christian community to people in depression, for which I am truly thankful. At that time, however, I had to suffer alone in silence, without being able to reach out to others. Knowing I would be misjudged or criticized, the only way I could cope was by living in outright denial.

As I continued my search for solutions, I grasped at every spiritual formula and resource I could find. I did believe in the "prayer of faith for healing" (James 5:14) and thought if I could just find the right person to pray for me, God would instantly make me well. I went through so many healing lines and had so many hands laid on me that I am surprised I had any hair left on my head.

Whenever I saw a Christian TV helpline number on the screen, I hurriedly dialed it and asked the counselor to pray a (yet another) prayer of healing for me. It seemed I was doing everything I knew to do, yet my depression was only getting worse.

Grasping at Straws

The person in depression tends to be impulsive and ready to grasp at almost any straw in an attempt to escape the feelings of hopelessness. With little ability to have spiritual discernment or to make logical decisions, the individual may look at prayer in a magical or mystical way, sometimes attaching it to special people, places, formulae, etc., rather than treating it as a biblical exercise in faith.

God's mercy cannot be overstated, and no one should be discouraged from seeking spiritual remedy, regardless of the problem. However, it should be pointed out that the person with an emotional disorder often becomes a victim of faulty thinking processes. The (spiritual) concept of walking in faith is often overridden by the (natural) obsession to escape the torment.

It certainly wasn't that I didn't believe God could do miracles. In my own family, I had witnessed God's healing touch on my sister when she accidentally drank poison as a little girl. God had also healed my grandfather of stomach cancer when the doctor had given him only six months to live. I had read the testimonies of others who had received miraculous instant healings from depression. So my heart was filled with even more heaviness and pain because I couldn't understand why God didn't heal me. After all, I thought, *Doesn't the scripture say*, God is no respecter of persons?

No Respecter of Person?

One scripture quoted often to Christians looking for a miracle is, "God is no respecter of persons." The implication is whatever God has done for one person, He will do the exact same thing for another. Whenever using scripture, however, it is important to keep it in proper context.

In speaking those words (Acts 10:34–35, KJV), Peter was expressing his surprise in discovering that God's gift of salvation had been made available not only to the Jews but also to the Gentiles. To take that one verse and make it into a blanket doctrinal statement is a failure to "rightly divide the word of truth" (2 Tim. 2:15, KJV).

Peter had learned earlier that God does not necessarily deal with everyone alike (John 21:20–22). Paul learned to accept (even with glory!) his "thorn in the flesh" (2 Cor. 12:7–10). Some in the Hall of Faith (Heb. 11) were delivered, some were not. The Bible is replete with examples of individuals who received individual fulfillment and wholeness but in completely different ways.

Remember, Satan can quote scripture too!

I now have come to understand how Satan tries to ship-wreck people's faith by trying to convince them that God doesn't care as much for them as He does for someone else. My heart goes out to those whose faith has been shattered because Satan was able to distort a truth from God's Word to their tormented and weary minds. We must take the whole Word of God and "rightly divide" it (2 Tim. 2:15). Later, I was able to understand that and realized that scriptural confusion was just a part of Satan's devious plan to destroy my faith.

When I did, however, finally see that Satan was tempting me to believe a lie, my mind frantically searched for another reason for my continued suffering. (My husband has often teased me about "always having to have a reason for everything," but I think a lot of people get into problems trying to figure everything out.) That is precisely why Proverbs 3:5 (KJV) tells us not to "lean unto (our) own understanding."

In the end of my crazy reasoning, I finally concluded that pride must be my problem. I tried to think of something I could do that might make me more humble. I had the mistaken idea that maybe I could earn my healing. Shortly after pinpointing pride as the culprit, I attended a ladies' retreat where the speaker was praying for the sick. As she prayed, many were being slain in the spirit. I thought, *Maybe this is my time*, and quickly got in line. Determined to do whatever it took to get my healing, I got "slain." I am still not sure whether it was the Spirit or the flesh, but I certainly did go down!

I had been taught that Naaman the leper had to be willing to dip in the muddy Jordan for his healing (2 Kings 5), and I reasoned that I needed to have my pride dipped, in order for God to help me. While it certainly may be true that God sometimes needs to deal with one's pride, I look back now and believe that it was probably just another straw held out for my eager grasp. Thank God, He knew my heart and overlooked my naïve but sincere attempts that seemed so reasonable to me at the time. But still, I was not healed, and in fact, my depression continued to worsen.

God always has a way, but sometimes, it includes waiting!

I tried to follow the spiritual advice offered by many others, but it only brought me more confusion. The truth was, though I had finally taken a step of faith by going to a doctor, that wasn't the way I wanted God to bring about my healing. I wanted Him to give me a miracle right then and there, with no further ado. So after the initial attempt to use my faith, I refused to follow through with the treatment prescribed to me. It took a while for me to learn that sometimes, faith involves staying the course before seeing any appreciable results.

I have heard it quoted that God has a pathway for your healing. It may not include what someone else has done or would do in your situation, but God knows our individual makeup and needs, and He designs and tailors for us a personal path of guidance. For me, the plan seemed to include being under a doctor's care and taking prescribed medication for my medical condition. I did not want to accept that plan, and I went through one of the biggest struggles of my life.

God wants us to keep our confidence and trust in Him no matter what instrument He may choose to bring our healing to us.

When I did take my prescribed medicine, I felt overwhelmed with guilt and condemnation. Satan took advantage of the situation and continuously distorted the truth of God's Word to me. For example, I had read in Philippians 3:3 (KJV) that believers are to "have no confidence in the flesh." Therefore, I concluded that God didn't want me to use medical means. That might seem like irrational thinking, but because of the debilitating effect the depression was having on my mind, I didn't have the ability to reason coherently or exercise normal thought processes.

My guilt was increased by plenty of well-meaning Christians who felt I should not use "those ol' pills" (as one friend described them). I wondered, "What if my taking the medicine is displeasing to God?" I earnestly wanted to do the right thing, but I continued to vacillate in my thinking. One moment, I would feel that taking the medicine was "leaning on the arm of flesh" and stop taking it. Then the next minute, I would think, *But I'm not supposed to be double-minded either,* and I would try once more to continue with the course prescribed by the doctor. Both those opposing thoughts are scriptural, in the right context, but Satan knows how to make Bible verses seem contradictory in order to bring confusion!

Besides being determined to settle for nothing less than immediate divine healing, I had other concerns about following the doctor's orders. I was afraid the medicine would have bad side effects, or that I was going to become addicted. In my perplexity, and not realizing that a lot of my irrational thinking was being further amplified by the depression, I finally concluded that God must not be in *any* of my choices because I was confused and the scripture says, "God is not the author of confusion, but of peace..." (1 Cor. 14:33, KJV). Again, Satan was using the Word against me to further torment my mind.

I share all this because I want to caution anyone who has been victimized by Satan's crazy twisting of scriptures as I was. He especially takes advantage of us when we are weary and exhausted. It is usually when our bodies and minds are tired that our faith becomes more vulnerable to Satan's attacks.

Most of my attempted shortcuts were nothing more than detours!

As previously stated, I would take my medicine one day and stop taking it the next. Looking back at this behavior, it is now kind of humorous to me. Because I'm such a perfectionist, I must have been trying to cover all my bases—just in case one of my actions turned out to be wrong. Of course, that erratic medical approach didn't produce a lot of positive results.

My thinking was just as erratic. One day, I would decide that with God helping me, I would try to be more consistent in what I was doing and believe as long as I was doing the best I could to follow His lead, He would continue to help me. Then the next day, I would decide that I must have made this mess, and now I had to get myself out of it.

It took me a long time and a lot of struggle to finally accept that God doesn't expect any more than that of which we are capable, and if we do stray from the path, He knows how to get us back on course. Whatever God is leading us to do, we need to do it in faith and stick with it no matter how we think or feel!

We are not always given to understand God's leadings.

Our faith must always reside in God first, rather than methods or expectations. Isaiah 55:8 KJV says, "For my thoughts are not your thoughts, neither are your ways my ways …." Also, Psalm 77:19 (KJV) says, "Thy way is in the sea, and thy path in the great waters, and thy footsteps are not known." We will not always be able to understand God's purposes, and I have noticed when I start thinking I have things all figured out, He will usually allow my little ducks to get knocked out of their row in order to keep me dependent on Him.

Whenever things started going in a negative direction, I would once again feel pushed to take matters into my own hands. The twenty-third Psalm doesn't say the shepherd *pushes* me. It says the shepherd *leads* me. It took me a long time to realize that just because everything seemed to be going haywire, that didn't necessarily mean that I had to try and fix it.

I undoubtedly birthed a thousand Ishmaels. That story is found in Genesis 16. And that, my friend, can make for a lot of dirty diapers to change! When we hatch up our own plans, it usually creates more problems for us as it did for Sarah when she concocted the scheme involving her husband and handmaiden.

For example, whenever I started on a different medication and didn't see the immediate results I wanted, I would feel I had to take a totally new direction right then, or things would really get out of control. It is amazing the stupid ideas that we can come up with! I (ignorantly) felt my whole recovery process was entirely up to me; and yet, to my dismay, I was incapable of finding an answer.

God was allowing me to experience my inability to control my circumstances in order that I might learn to wait upon the Lord and place my faith in Him alone.

To obtain more positive results, I had to learn to stay the course. It was very difficult for me to wait patiently for God to work. My husband would often tell me, "You have to be patient." But patience had never been one of my strong points, even before the depression. The scripture, though, kept reminding me that I must continue to hope and believe God's Word. It said that if I would be patient, there would be a reward. Hebrews 10:36 reminded me, "Ye have need of patience, that, after ye have done the will of God, ye might receive the promise" (KJV). And God knows how to teach us patience, if we will learn. Sometimes, of course, that means we must wait for God's timing for His Word of promise to be fulfilled.

God always has a specific purpose when I'm forced to wait!

One of the lessons I learned is, God sometimes "makes us lie down," in order to "restore our souls" (Ps. 23, KJV). We usually don't appreciate those down times, but they are needed so that our bodies and minds may be refreshed. God was stretching my faith and, at the same time, was allowing me to witness His faithfulness to me. I had to practice being still and learn what waiting really meant.

Waiting is often the only way that we can receive God's answers. That was difficult for me because it meant I had to let go of the reins of my life and let Christ be in complete control. It meant that I had to disengage myself from a somewhat vicious cycle of activity and ministry. Before the depression, I had always been a very active person, and my life was a lot like Martha's in the New Testament: I was busy, busy, busy. I had never allowed myself to be still without feeling guilty. I felt that working hard in ministry must surely be what pleased God most.

The Need for Balance

If Satan can't make us lazy or unconcerned, he will do his best to push us too far to the other extreme. Our "work for the Lord" can, in time, take the place of our "relationship with the Lord." That can be detrimental to our spiritual life in two ways:

First, we may become victims to the sin of pride in our efforts and accomplishments "for the Kingdom"; and secondly, we can (unconsciously) begin to think it is our works that make us pleasing to God rather than our faithfulness. (And there is a difference.)

However, aside from the spiritual implications, there are also other factors to consider. Our work for the Lord cannot be relegated only to ministerial or religious obligations. It also includes time spent with family and friends and time for ourselves. We sometimes hear church workaholics state, "I'd rather burn out than rust out!" The fact is, we do not have to do either. Living according to scriptural balance, we can be fruitful and productive in God's kingdom until our earthly course is completed.

The Crucible of Suffering

God sometimes has to "hedge (us) in so that (we) cannot get out" (Lam. 3:7, NKJV). As God began forcing me to wait, I found the time to seek Him with a new intensity. I soon discovered that I didn't have the strength to wait, so I was driven to seek Christ to ask for an impartation of supernatural strength from Him. I had been placed into a crucible of suffering that, at times, almost brought me to the brink of despair. But just when I thought I couldn't go any further, God would suddenly step into my situation and provide a strength I never thought possible.

In the beginning, I had tremendous fears. Later, as God enabled me to start relinquishing control of my life (and let Him be God), my fears slowly began to dissipate and be replaced with a greater trust. I love the story of Paul as it unfolds in Acts 27. Verse 20 (kjv) says, "All hope that we should be saved was then taken away." But then, verses 22–24 says that they were not to worry because, "There stood by me this night the angel of God…saying fear not…." While they were still in the midst of the storm, Paul had the assurance they would be saved.

We all have some type of weakness.

Many people—even Christians—feel that clinical depression is a result of personal weakness or failure, and that depressed people are undeserving of human support or God's intervention. The fact is, everyone has weaknesses that must be turned over to God in order to receive His help. At another time, Paul recognized that God could take his weakness and, through it, impart His divine strength. God plainly spoke to him, "My grace is sufficient for thee: for my strength is made perfect in weakness" (2 Cor. 12:9, kjv). The apostle was then able to respond:

> Most gladly therefore will I rather glory in my infirmities, that the power of Christ may rest upon me. Therefore I take pleasure in infirmities, in reproaches, in necessities, in persecutions, in dis-

tresses for Christ's sake: for when I am weak, then am I strong. (2 Cor. 12:9–10, KJV)

When he was pressed beyond measure, Paul had learned that God would be faithful to offer him either a way of escape or give him the power to endure. When God chooses not to extricate us from our difficulties, but instead, gives us the strength to carry on, it is *not* to be looked upon as weakness. Rather, it is an expression of His grace and strength that will shine through us to others.

"I had fainted unless I had believed to see the goodness of the Lord in the land of the living" (Ps. 27:13, KJV).

I had to choose to believe in God's goodness, or I honestly don't think I would have survived. Scripture teaches us that hope is a powerful anchor for our soul (Heb. 6:19). It is never God's desire for us to despair. No matter how weak we may feel, He throws out a lifeline to keep us from sinking under our adversity. David describes this when he said, "You have delivered my life from death, my eyes from tears, and my feet from stumbling and falling" (Ps. 116:8 AMP). Somehow God helped me to hope, but I still had many times when I would *feel* that things were, indeed, hopeless. In those dark moments, I had to remind myself that God was still there even though I didn't know where.

I learned to recall Psalm 66:8–10 (AMP), where David said, "Bless our God, O peoples, give Him grateful thanks and make the voice of His praise be heard, Who put and kept us among the living, and has not allowed our feet to slip."

I often have prayed, "Lord, please don't allow my feet to slip."

"Do not think it strange concerning the fiery trial..." (1 Pet. 4:12, NKJV).

While I was still grasping at every straw, I continued to wonder why I was singled out, or what I had done, to bring about my condition. That type of thinking had led only to more frustration and confusion. In time, I learned that there does not have to be a specific reason or cause for clinical depression. Sometimes, it just happens for seemingly no apparent reason.

Is It My Nerves?

It seems logical that a *nervous breakdown* (which is a term often applied to *major depression*) can be caused by built-up stress and pressure. Therefore, many people assume that depression and prior problems or unresolved emotional conflicts go hand in hand.

Depression does involve the nervous system—the chemical makeup and interaction of neurons—but is not necessarily caused by outside forces or faulty thinking

---

patterns. Undoubtedly, in some cases, stress and burnout are definite factors. Sometimes, depression can be a secondary condition in conjunction with another physical ailment. Often, there seems to be no apparent cause at all.

There may be a genetic factor involved as well. It is possible that some people have a predisposition toward depression. Many of those individuals never suffer any episodes of clinical depression while others do. Some event or problem may trigger the condition.

The important thing to remember is that depression (or any emotional disorder) is a medical condition, and nothing to be ashamed of.

Trials are just a part of living and don't always have to have a reason.

Later, when I did receive further diagnoses (which verified my condition), it was concluded that my problems stemmed from a neurological chemical imbalance with no apparent secondary cause.

Most people in depression may receive benefit from some form of competent counseling. Since my condition was not diagnosed as a result of past hurts or abuse, the counseling I received was mainly just to help keep me encouraged. (Having said that, let me clarify that, like anyone, I am sure there were things in my life that required repentance, forgiveness, and healing; but basically, my depression seemed to stem from a medical disorder alone.)

One thing I learned through my pain is that condemnation and criticism from others did not seem to be at all beneficial in my recovery. This is especially true for a person who is already struggling with nothing but negative feelings already. I have also come to believe that God doesn't kick us in the teeth when we are already down. He is there with forgiveness, emotional healing, or whatever encouragement a person might need (Phil. 4:19). Sadly, it has been rightly said, "Christians are the only ones who shoot their wounded." I say that because it was usually church people who gave me the most criticism during that time.

God is more willing to give than we are to receive.

I do believe God wants to bring wholeness to His children, but I have learned that His strength is available only as I am willing to turn to Him. It sure took a lot of pressure off me when I finally realized that for anything to be changed or fixed in me, God would have to do it. All He was asking of me was my willingness to trust, submit, and wait. Like Abraham, I had to learn to be patient and come to realize that my grasping at straws would not produce the Isaac I so desperately desired.

Checking Up

✓ When we are immersed in overwhelming personal problems, we may often feel God has forsaken us.

✓ We can easily become confused when we try to listen to everyone else's advice about our situation.

✓ Every believer's faith will be tested, and there will be those times when we just don't understand what God is doing.

✓ Grasping at straws is usually a human effort that turns into an endless and fruitless search.

✓ Satan's ultimate aim is to destroy our trust and faith in God.

✓ There are some spiritual principles that won't necessarily work in every situation.

✓ Satan will try to destroy our faith by making us think that God loves someone else more than He loves us.

✓ We may not always find a *reason* for our trial or difficulty.

✓ We need to learn the discipline of *being still* by patiently waiting on God.

✓ God can use our weaknesses in order for us to learn dependence upon Him.

✓ In counseling others, it is good to remember that restoration and emotional healing will require much encouragement and affirmation.

3

JOB'S COMFORTERS

Now when Job's three friends heard of all this evil
that was come upon him they came every one from
his own place ... to comfort him.

—Job 2:11 (AMP)

HOW CAN A person be comforted when there are so many
of us idiots around? I remember clearly the day I told my
ladies' Bible study group, "You know, I just don't believe
that Christians should ever have nerve problems!"

The greatest irony of all is that I made that statement
only about two weeks before I collapsed. Like many others
(before and since), I had said those words in complete igno-
rance. But the truth was, at the time, it was easier to deny
my own problem than to deal with it. *Denial* had become
the only coping mechanism that I knew how to use.

Sooner or later, we all need to confront our problems!

To keep from having to face my own condition, I stayed as busy as possible, trying to pretend that the depression did not exist. I hoped it would somehow go away. However, I could only do that for so long a time until exhaustion finally won the struggle, and I slowly ceased to function. I could no longer control my thoughts or think clearly. I was tormented with negative, destructive thoughts. I just wanted to die.

It was at that point that I began having suicidal thoughts. Death would be an escape from the pain that was relentlessly crippling me, and I couldn't see that it would make that much difference if my life were ended. I thought perhaps I already was in hell, so what I did no longer mattered. As I look back, I can easily identify with David in Psalm 124:1–3 when he sang, "If it had not been for God on my side, I would have perished in my affliction" (my paraphrase). I know now that the prayers of those who loved me sustained me through this severe time of temptation.

I was unsure about my salvation. I tried to pray, but I just couldn't. I felt completely forsaken by the Almighty, in spite of reading the scripture that plainly said, "If I ascend up into heaven, thou art there: if I make my bed in hell, behold, thou art there" (Ps. 139:8, KJV).

Even though the Scripture makes it clear God is with us no matter where we are, I could no longer grasp its meaning. My mind simply no longer functioned. I felt like I was drowning in a bottomless pit with no way out.

When I was at the point of drowning, God somehow kept me afloat!

I tried to believe God was still with me, but for all practical purposes, I had physically, mentally, and emotionally shut down. I could feel absolutely nothing. For nearly a year, I suffered through sleepless nights and days that were filled with panic attacks. I had no appetite for food. I grew restless and found it impossible to concentrate or relax.

As I grew worse, it became difficult for me to carry on a normal conversation. I sometimes left my house and later found that I didn't know where I was or what I was doing there. Finally, I would be able to gather my mental faculties sufficiently in order to find a phone and call my husband. He would then have to come to wherever I was and take me home.

If you want to be an encourager, don't gasp, gawk, or wail!

The seriousness of my condition had become apparent to everyone around me. I had always been a very active person, and it was quite difficult for other people to see me or accept my weakened state. I do remember receiving some very startled looks from some! It reminds me of Job's friends when they first saw him after his calamities hit:

> When they saw Job from a distance, they scarcely recognized him. Wailing loudly, they tore their robes and threw dust into the air over their heads to demonstrate their grief. Then they sat on the ground with him for seven days and nights. (Job 2:13 New Living Translation)

This verse is really kind of funny if you stop to think about it. They were supposed to be encouragers! Brother, who needs enemies when you have encouragers that are going to gawk at you, gasp, and even wail! I remember many onlookers who said to me, "You really look terrible," or, "What in the world are you going to do?"

Now I would like to insert a little bit of common-sense wisdom here. It would really help all would-be comforters to respond to negative situations with a few words of faith or, at least, something sort of positive. Gasping and staring at one in desperate need tends to dampen that person's faith a little! If people can't say something positive, at least they should silently ask the Lord to help them do no further damage.

Eventually, the day came when I no longer had enough energy to go out in public at all. My days and nights were spent sitting and staring into space, doing absolutely nothing. It was then that my fierce struggle against accepting medical treatment came to an end.

The first hospitalization

I allowed myself to be admitted to the local county hospital. I had gone almost a year with very little normal sleep, and my situation had become quite serious. The doctors tried all the usual medical procedures and techniques to induce regular sleep, but nothing worked. That alone was a frightening experience. I knew I was not responding to any of the medication, and it wasn't long before I began to give up all hope for recovery. After fifteen days with no success, the doctors decided to move me to the psychiatric ward at Vanderbilt University Hospital in Nashville where I could receive specialized treatment.

Yet another hospital!

Upon entry onto the psychiatric floor, I was led to a secluded ward behind locked doors. It almost felt like I was being ushered into prison. Due to the seriousness of my condition, I was placed in a special room (no glass mirrors, no sharp edges, etc.) to keep me from harming myself. Though I had consciously considered that death would be a relief, I had not actually seriously contemplated taking my life at that point.

As horrendous as that season in my life was, I can certainly testify now that God was truly "my strength, my fortress, my refuge in the day of affliction" (Jer. 16:19, NKJV).

The psychiatric facility, which had become my new home, was one that was shared with others who had various emotional or mental disorders. I was given a routine each day that I had to follow.

My day began at 6:00 a.m. when the nurse came in to tell me to get up and take a shower. I cannot begin to relate how difficult that was for me. My body was so tired; I thought I would absolutely die just to follow that simple order. Many do not realize how one's emotional state can affect his or her physical strength. For a person in major depression, the physical exhaustion and accompanying pains can be truly indescribable.

All I wanted to do was just lie there and never move again.

She'll die if we don't do something immediately!

Normally, antidepressant medication typically takes a few days to build up in the system in order to have an optimum effect. Also, it may take some trial and error to find a medication that will be effective for the individual situation. So it often takes time for patients to respond positively to treatment. As a result of my lengthy sleep deprivation and emotional and physical exhaustion, whatever medications that had been tried had brought no positive results. I had lost nearly one hundred pounds and was like a lifeless zombie.

The head psychiatrist at Vanderbilt explained the situation to my husband. "Your wife is critically ill," he said. "We feel her only hope for recovery is electroconvulsive treatments." So as a last resort, they put me through a series of shock treatments (ECT) to keep me alive. Years later, a neurologist assured me that at that point I did, indeed, have the cancer of all depression.

Electroconvulsive Therapy (ECT)

Electroconvulsive Therapy (ECT) remains a controversial treatment for clinical depression. Much of the negative attitude toward ECT is because of the brutality associated with the procedure a half-century ago.

Today, ECT is administered in several low-voltage doses while the patient is anesthetized and closely monitored. Generally, there are no long-term side effects.

While improvements in antidepressant medication have lessened the need for ECT, the therapy is still con-

---

sidered by many mental health professionals to be a viable alternative treatment in the most severe cases.

Medical science continues to experiment with other types of treatment. For instance, Transcranial Magnetic Stimulation (TMS) is a new treatment that stimulates nerve cells in the brain by moving a handheld electric coil over the scalp. Some believe that TMS—or similar new therapies—will one day eliminate the need for ECT.

The prayers of God's people were continually being made for me at that time, and the ECT did seem to stabilize my condition. Throughout my long road to recovery, God never abandoned me. Hebrews 13:5 (NKJV) declares, "He will never leave (us) or forsake (us)," and even though at times we may not sense that God is there, He will remain faithful to his Word.

It seemed like an eternity before I began to notice any real change. Every day, I continued to respond reluctantly to the discipline of a daily schedule. I could not see the rationale behind forcing me to mobilize myself when I was so exhausted, but I did make an attempt to follow the program.

Even small steps are important for recovery.

Those small steps seemed so insignificant at the time, but it is important to keep in mind that anything a person in depression can be encouraged to do is a positive step toward recovery. I must honestly say, however, that for me, the process was long and difficult, and most of the time, I just wanted to quit. With support from the doctor and my husband and family, my strength did begin to improve little by little as I was encouraged and coached to cooperate.

Sometimes, a bad memory isn't such a bad thing!

It took a much longer period of time for my mind to begin functioning again. I still found it difficult to concentrate and often just stared into space. Later, I learned that I did not even recognize my twelve-year-old daughter when she came to visit me in the hospital. That was a very difficult time for her because she could not understand all that was happening. I am thankful that I do not remember much of what transpired during that time. I think that may be a pretty good perspective to take at times concerning our past!

And then came the gloom-and-doom encouragers!

There are some things, however, that I *do* remember. I recall Job's comforters!

I believe I now have a pretty good definition for these choice people: a Job's comforter is someone you wish had never been given the opportunity to make you feel better. I have discovered that if you feel bad *before* their visit, you *really* will feel bad afterward.

It's better to say nothing than to cause a person to lose hope!

I realize now that many people simply did not know how to respond to someone in my condition. But looking back, I wish they had known how to exercise a little more Godly wisdom or at least a little common sense.

A few of those visitors I remember well. One individual told me I just needed to "snap out of it." Well, if I could have, I would have. I certainly didn't want to be in the condition I was in, and if there had been a "snapping out of it" line, I would have been at the front of it.

In those days, there weren't too many in the church world who had a great deal of compassion or patience with those suffering from emotional disorders. It seemed that a lot of people tended to separate afflictions into two different categories as if to say, "Well, it's okay if you have heart problems, and it's okay if you have diabetes. We'll stand by you and pray for you. But depression? Really!" The fact that clinical depression is as much of a medical condition as any other disease seemed foreign to them.

When one assigns to another the entire blame for his or her depression, it can place a tremendous burden of guilt and hopelessness upon the sufferer (who already feels like the biggest loser ever). At that time, I simply did not have the ability to bring myself to a more positive attitude or to (as was suggested) snap out of it. My mind was so weary I couldn't control my thought patterns even if I had wanted to and so it continued to race on and on, never shutting off. At that time, I could not even think in terms of having a positive mind-set. As a person improves, he or she is eventually able to have a more positive outlook, but those in deep depression—outside of a miracle—are not usually able to do that.

Degrees of Depression

Not everyone who is diagnosed with depression has the exact same symptoms or suffers to the same degree. The type of depression—according to its severity—normally determines the type and duration of treatment.

Some victims require medication for months or years, some for only a short time, and some (suffering from milder cases) recover without the aid of medical intervention.

People who do not understand the nature of depression often try to motivate the sufferer to think or act in a normal way, not realizing that the abnormal neuron/chemical interactions in the brain won't allow normal thinking patterns.

We need to offer affirmations instead of accusations.

And then there was the comforter who looked down her spiritual nose at me and said, "Well, if you'd just have more faith, your depression would go away." Even if a lack of faith had been a part of the equation, her words left me feeling totally void and hopeless. Regardless of the reason one may be suffering, it seems to me that the best counsel would be to speak a few words of faith to the desperate person who already feels victimized by his or her condition.

We all need kind words!

One thing the person in depression does understand is reassurance. He or she may not always seem to respond to encouragement, but to the person in the depths of despair, the slightest ray of hope can make all the difference in the world. It is not unusual for those in depression to require almost constant reassurance, until they are able to retain it by themselves.

Then came the fault-finding encouragers.

These were the comforters who were quick to tell me that sin was the cause of my sickness. They began first by picking my family apart, trying to find someone or something on which to place the blame. Then they started on me. Since I did not have the ability to discern the validity of these comments, I repented of every sin I had ever committed, just hoping that if they were right, maybe God would quit being angry at me.

Satan doesn't play fair. He likes to get us on his merry-go-rounds!

Let me make it clear that God did deal with me about a lot of issues as I was recovering. There were things that I wanted God not only to *cleanse*, but to *change* in my life. Having said that, however, I also had to learn that when Satan got me on His *merry-go-round* of *accusations*, it usually turned into an endless witch hunt, leaving me feeling that my repentance was never quite adequate, and surely, there must be *one more sin* I hadn't remembered.

This is probably hard for nonsufferers to understand because we've largely been taught that as Christians, we will always feel at peace when our hearts are right before God. But at the time, I didn't have any peace or positive feelings about anything. Since we should not base our salvation on feelings, I realized that in order to survive, I had to *choose* to start believing God's Word—whether or not I *felt* like I was forgiven. Thank God, "If we confess our sins, He is faithful and just to forgive us our sins, and to cleanse us from all unrighteousness" (1 John 1:9, KJV). We must learn to take God at His Word.

Taking God at His Word is the foundation for our learning to walk by faith.

God never leaves us victims of the enemy. I believe whenever Satan backs us into a corner, God is still right there with us. The Apostle Paul, one of the greatest saints who ever lived, believed that those who hold to God's promises can be victorious in any kind of trial.

> We are troubled on every side, yet not distressed; we are perplexed, but not in despair; persecuted, but not forsaken; cast down, but not destroyed. (2 Cor. 4:8–9, KJV)

Jeremiah 32:27 (KJV) says, "Behold, I am the Lord, the God of all flesh: is there any thing too hard for me?" I am so thankful that whenever those times of trouble have occurred, God always eventually comes through with help of some kind.

And here is one of Satan's favorites!

During some of my darkest days, I reasoned that I must have committed the unpardonable sin. I felt condemned by my shortcomings and overwhelmed by my physical and emotional weakness. I thought perhaps I had just messed up too often, and now God had tired of forgiving me.

Many people have suffered that kind of tormenting thought when they no longer have a sense of God's presence. But it was then that I made another new discovery: God's Word in a situation is equal to his presence. One wonderful thing about trials is that we are given the opportunity to discover what we don't know or haven't practiced in a long time. It was during those times that I slowly began to learn the importance of *not* living according to my feelings.

I also discovered that Satan is deceptive and that he is "the accuser of the brethren" (Rev. 12:10, KJV). He is the master at bringing undeserved guilt and condemnation and does his best to convince believers that his accusations are true. In fact, the New International Version of that scripture describes him as "The accuser of our brothers, who accuses them before our God day and night." That means he never lets up on us! Thank God, though, that verse also reminds us that there is coming a time in which Satan will forever be cast down. I had to learn simply to accept God's forgiveness by faith and *make the choice* to believe His Word.

Feelings can be so very deceptive. In her book *Choosing to Cope*, Mary Beggs recounts her depression experience by saying,

> My feelings were real, but I had to recognize them as feelings only—which did not always correspond to fact. Because I refused to give up and because in faith I read and recited God's Word consistently, I was one day able to choose what it says about His strength being in the believer rather than accept the emotions and feelings that ruled me.[1]

Words are powerful weapons that can be used to hurt or heal!

Evil reports are everywhere, and you can be sure that Satan always has someone who will tell you that they know someone who had your ailment and ended up dying from it. It seems that some people's primary mission in life is to be the bearer of bad tidings. Many, many times I have had to claim Psalm 112:7 (NKJV) where it says, "He will not be afraid of evil tidings; His heart is steadfast; trusting in the Lord." It seemed that everywhere I turned, something or someone was always there to discourage my faith.

Did you say comforter?

I'll never forget one night after church when we were at a restaurant having a meal with a guest preacher. He was a number-one example of what we shouldn't say when we don't know what to say. We began sharing with him a little about my depression. What a mistake that turned out to be! He responded by telling me about a preacher's wife he had known "with that condition" who was "still in a mental ward somewhere."

That preacher will never know the grief that he brought to my already fragile emotions. I know he did not realize that I was not fully recovered or how his untimely words brought immeasurable torture to my heart and mind.

His remarks continued to ring on and on in my mind. You see, prior to that conversation, Satan had already started painting a picture in my head of me being locked away permanently in a mental ward somewhere. Satan does know who to use and how best to upset us! I desperately dug into the Word for some kind of encouragement. (At least I was learning to go to a reliable source.) One day, while reading the Bible, God spoke to me through Psalm 140:7 (NKJV). David said, "O God the Lord, the strength of my salvation, you have covered my head in the day of battle." Through that verse, God gave me a much-needed assurance that even though at times I felt like I was going crazy, He could somehow put a protective covering over my mind. I have been able to encourage many sufferers of depression with this verse of scripture as they have been tormented by those same thoughts.

A word aptly spoken is like apples of gold in a setting of silver. (Prov. 25:11, NIV)

In spite of the "evil comforters," God did send me individuals who were ready to speak a *good* word to my fainting spirit. One such encouraging word came from a lady who had gone through a similar depression experience such as I had. At that time, I was lying in bed in an almost catatonic state, empty and feeling nothing. Her face actually lit up when she saw me as though to make me aware that she completely understood my condition. She looked at me and said, "Chris, I know it looks dark now, but there's light at the end of the tunnel." As she spoke those words of encouragement, I felt a tear trickle down my cheek.

She had indeed brought me some real hope! It wasn't that she had changed my situation or even given me an understandable explanation of things; however, she had ignited within me the first flicker of hope in a very long time! As Proverbs 18:21 (NKJV) states, "Death and life are in the power of the tongue."

Jesus is the model for encouragers!

Jesus always ministered life to those who were hurting. He didn't critique and analyze them to see if He thought they might be worthy of His encouragement. He simply came to heal the broken hearted (Isa. 61:1). Sometimes, we think of healing only as it applies to the physical. Jesus, however, came to bring healing to *the whole person.* That not only includes the physical; it relates to the emotional and mental as well.

If we are going to be real encouragers, it is vital that we show compassion by what we say regardless of what kinds of needs are present in individuals' lives. Proverbs 12:18 brings validity to that thought by reminding us, "There are those who speak rashly, like the piercing of a sword, but the tongue of the wise brings healing" (AMP).

Regarding the evil reports brought to me by bad encouragers, God was showing me to not be *ignorant of Satan's devices* and teaching me to discern that most of those messages really weren't from God. That is a lesson I have had to relearn many, many times.

Did you say, "A word from the Lord?"

In conversation with a new beautician in our town, I had briefly shared with her some of my struggles with clinical depression. I attempted to tell her that God had brought me a long way, but that I still was looking to Christ and believing him for complete healing.

Looking back, I think probably my reason for sharing with that total stranger was just an attempt to encourage myself. At that time, I was going through a particularly difficult low cycle. I realize now that what I was looking for was a word of affirmation from her that I was going to make it. Was I in for a shocker!

The next day, I heard a knock at my front door and was quite surprised to see the lady standing there. She proceeded to tell me that God had shown her in a dream that I needed to be delivered from demons. I have no doubt that she felt she had brought me a wonderful message of hope and cheer! Instead of comfort, her so-called *word* sent me into a state of gloom, despair, and agony!

But the firm foundation of (laid by) God stands, sure and unshaken. (2 Tim. 2:19 AMP)

Immediately, I went to the Word and began looking up scriptures concerning this subject matter. I began by reading the verse that says, "Greater is he that is in you than he that is in the world" (1 John 4:4, KJV). I continued to look up more passages in an attempt to establish my faith, but it seemed her words continued to haunt me. Finally, after being thoroughly discouraged and tormented by her comments, I asked my husband if he thought that I might need deliverance. I believe, according to 1 Corinthians 11:3, that God gives us our husbands for a covering.

My husband patiently began going through the scripture with me concerning that subject. In the end, I realized that Satan had tried to bring this discouragement and fear into my heart to make me question Christ's saving and keeping power. The scripture helped me see that we, as believers, are not to be fearful but are given an incorruptible inheritance that does not fade away, which is reserved in heaven for all "who are kept by the power of God through faith unto salvation" (1 Pet. 1:5, NKJV).

Mental Illness and Demonic Possession

There has been a great deal of controversy over whether or not Christians can be possessed by the devil. Some have pointed to certain experiences to bolster their arguments that believers can be demonized. The light of scripture, however, reveals no evidence that the forces of Satan and the Spirit of Christ can coexist in the same dwelling. There are many passages that mark the division between the presence of God and the work of the devil, and it would seem contradictory for the enemy of the Almighty to live within the temple of the Holy Spirit (1 Cor. 3:16–17, 23). We do, of course, know that Satan comes to press and oppress every saint of God whenever he can.

Because of the mysteries of emotional and mental disorders, there have always been those who blame such things on demonic activity. (By *mysteries* we mean that there is no fever, swelling, or other tangible symptoms such as are present when dealing with most physical infirmities.)

We certainly believe that there are *real* demonic attacks upon people today and even demonic possession; however, it is safe to say that *most* mental/emotional problems should not be blamed on demons. Doing so just brings more fear and unsettledness to the already-distressed victim. It is important that both spiritual discernment and wisdom be used in our attempts to help those needing healing from *any* kind of sickness or torment.

The End of Her Story

An interesting twist to the story is that a short time after this experience, the lady who gave me her "word from the Lord" left her husband for another man because she said God had "given her a word" to do so. That brought home an important lesson to my heart: a person suffering from depression is so eager to receive encouragement that he or she can become an easy target for the "I have a word for you" type of person. But not everyone who seems to be spiritual is sent our way with heavenly credentials. I had to learn to be cautious about opening up to certain people.

God may allow even those we love to fail us so that our focus and trust remain completely on Him.

I do want to make it clear that God has used some wonderful people at different times to encourage me. Those individuals always brought me hope, encouragement, and sometimes instruction. Their words seemed to be God-breathed and brought confirmation, encouragement, and peace to my heart.

On the other hand, there have been times when the well-meant efforts of people of integrity and proven relationships with God proved futile. I believe God allowed those disappointing experiences to happen whenever I started looking too much to individuals, instead of keeping my focus and trust on God alone.

My family had always been very supportive, but there were times when even they failed to offer the support I thought I needed. But thank God, even when others fail, He has promised to be there to help us. Psalm 27:10 says, "Even if my father and mother abandon me, the Lord will hold me close" (NLT). And He is indeed a real "friend who sticks closer than a brother" (Prov. 18:24, NKJV).

God is a good comforter.

A good biblical illustration of how God deals with us is seen in the life of Elijah. This mightily-used prophet was undoubtedly suffering from emotional and physical burn-out. He was discouraged and depressed. Ironically, on the heels of a great victory, he ran in fear from Jezebel. (Probably not a bad idea, she was one vicious woman!) After such a great battle with the priests of Baal and running fast and far from that evil queen, Elijah found himself spiritually and physically exhausted.

I have heard many preachers condemn Elijah for his emotional letdown, but I don't find God "tarring and feathering" him for his weakness. Instead, God sent an angel to minister to him (1 Kings 19:4–8). After Elijah had rested, the angel even baked him an angel food cake! (Well, it sounds like a spiritually-infused cake to me because the scripture says he went in the strength of that meal forty days and forty nights. Now that was some cake!) God knew Elijah was exhausted, and He ministered to both his emotional and physical needs. Then after food, rest, and some time alone with God, Elijah recovered and went on serving the Lord.

God did supply all my needs according to His wonderful riches in glory!

God was so good to me, even amidst all the confusion and pain, and somehow He was able to get through to me the kind of help I needed.

My "comforters"—both good and bad—came and went, and at last the day came . . . when the hospital released me to go home.

Checking Up

- ✓ To keep from facing our problems, we often choose denial or some other escape method in order not to deal with it.
- ✓ We sometimes have to come to the end of ourselves before we will accept the help we need.

- ✓ Quite often, the response of other people to our problems can be a discouragement to our faith.
- ✓ Progress usually takes time, and we must be willing to take even the smallest steps.
- ✓ Even when we feel we can no longer face the challenges of everyday living, it does not mean that God has abandoned us.
- ✓ We need to learn not to be a "Job's comforter," and we need to give encouragement and solutions instead of criticism and blame.
- ✓ Taking God at His Word is the essence of walking by faith, which is walking by his Word and not by our feelings.
- ✓ Satan will send accusations and lies in an attempt to defeat us.
- ✓ We have to learn not to listen to evil reports.
- ✓ A good encourager is one who brings healing and encouragement with a heart of compassion.
- ✓ It is important to get a good understanding of our position of righteousness as a child of God.
- ✓ It is good to let others help us, but we must always remember God is our one true source of help above all else.

PART II

THE BREAKING

And the vessel that he made of clay was marred
in the hand of the potter; so he made it again into
another vessel, as it seemed good to the potter
to make.

—Jeremiah 18:4 (NKJV)

4

KICKING AGAINST THE PRICKS

And he fell to the earth, and heard a voice saying
unto him, Saul, Saul, why persecutest thou me?
And he said, Who art thou, Lord? And the Lord
said, I am Jesus whom thou persecutest: it is hard
for thee to kick against the pricks.

—Acts 9:4–5 (KJV)

"HONEY, YOU CAN fight against your situation all you want, but all you are doing is *kicking against the pricks*." Those are the exact words my husband spoke to me during my struggle with depression. However, it was a powerful truth that I could not get away from. I often found myself so frustrated about my situation that I just wanted to scream and run! (Though for the life of me, I don't know where I would have run.) Even though I had improved after coming home from the hospital, I was still a long way from recovery.

Before my hospitalization, all the fight had literally gone out of me. I was in a physical and mental state of total exhaustion. But now that I had begun to improve, I quickly returned to what I knew how to do best, and that was to continue fighting against everything about my situation that I didn't like. I fought against my condition, my medicine, and my doctors. I hated being sick and found it very difficult to accept the fact that all of my health issues had not instantly been eliminated.

Running from the Truth

If people don't grasp at straws trying to find the secret of instant recovery, they often try to *escape* or *ignore* their painful situations by immersing themselves in activities that allow them (at least temporarily) to avoid the reality of their circumstances. In the long run, it only creates more problems.

Denial may seem to work for a while, but sooner or later, the crash always comes.

My fighting was not the good fight of faith!

Instead of being grateful that I was somewhat better, I held on to impatience and dissatisfaction. I not only wanted my life to be normal; I wanted it to be *better* than normal! I'll never forget my dear mother's statement to me: "Honey, you need to learn to be thankful for what God has already done for you." I was acting like a spoiled child who cannot be happy unless everything goes his or her way.

I am reminded of the Israelites who were always complaining about something. As I studied about God's response to their attitude, I realized how much this displeased and angered Him. It seemed like every time God supplied one of their needs, they found something else to gripe about.

I did not realize that I (along with the Israelites) was creating within myself a vicious cycle of restlessness that was nothing more than utter rebellion against God. And as I stubbornly kicked against the goads (things beyond my control), I could not enjoy the life God had begun giving back to me. Paul had evidently learned to trust in God's sovereignty over his life when he wrote, "I have learned, in whatsoever state I am, therewith to be content" (Phil. 4:11, KJV). I believe the apostle probably experienced the *results* of discontent as he fought against present circumstances. (We are given to understand that he had to *learn*.) Paul had to be brought to the realization that discontentment would always steal any enjoyment of the moment.

I was absolutely making myself miserable with my ungrateful attitude. But for the person experiencing clinical depression, it is very difficult to be thankful about anything, especially when it is almost impossible to process and understand the dynamics of the condition.

I was only inflicting more pain on myself by my persistent kicking.

When we disregard God and determine to bring about our own outcome, we usually end up inflicting even more pain on ourselves and others as well. Long ago, Isaiah let us know the dangers of such self-will: "Woe to him that strives with his Maker! Shall the clay say to him who forms it, 'What are you making?' Or shall your handiwork say, 'He has no hands?'" (Isa. 45:9, NKJV). I finally realized I had to *choose* to believe that God really did know what He was doing in my life, and then *choose* to cooperate with Him.

God's prods are often the only thing that keeps us going forward.

In Paul's day, animals were driven to their destination with long goads, which had sharpened ends. If an animal chose to kick against the pricks, the sharp point would jab into his body. If the animal continued to fight or kick, it would only inflict more pain on itself. The only remedy for the pain would be to cooperate with the prod as the animal was urged to move forward.

I didn't realize it at the time, but God often uses divine goads (the tool of trouble) to bring us to where He wants us to be. Those heavenly goads keep us from becoming complacent and willing to settle for the status quo and direct us in the desired path. It is through prayerful submission that we discover the divine plan unfolding. This truth is illustrated even in the life of Christ as the writer of Hebrews says, "Though He was a Son, yet he learned obedience by the things which He suffered" (Heb. 5:8, NKJV).

That unfolding plan can be clearly seen in the life of the Apostle Paul. When God struck him down and made him blind, he (then referred to as "Saul") responded by saying, "Lord, what do you want me to do?" (Acts 9:6). (Read the entire account in Acts 9.) As a result of his surrender to God, his sight returned as Ananias prayed for him.

I see a comparison here with my own life during those times when I kicked against the pricks. As long as I remained self-willed, my spiritual eyes remained blind. Spiritual sight only returned when I yielded my will and stopped fighting against God's prods. When we are obedient and open to God, He will make His path plain to us.

I love the scripture that says, "Commit your way to the Lord, trust also in Him, and He shall bring it to pass" (Ps. 37:5, NKJV). When we can say, "Lord, what would you have me to do?" it gets us started on the right track. I, of course, have to say *started* because unfortunately, there have been times when I have had to surrender and recommit my way to God again and again. Perhaps that is due to the fact that even though I wanted to be obedient, I was not always wholehearted about it. *Self* still wanted its way.

It's hard to go forward when we're digging in our heels!

Since I couldn't see God's finished master plan, my surrender was often halfhearted at best. I had the idea that God could not work in my life unless He first removed my need for medication. God had to show me that he could work in any situation no matter how difficult it seemed to me. The Lord asked His prophet, "Is there anything too hard for Me?" (Jer. 32:27, NKJV). That verse speaks volumes to anyone who believes God needs our direction before He can do His job.

What About Medication?

Some Christians are convinced that taking any kind of medication is showing a lack of faith in God's ability to heal. Others believe that God is the author of true science and that medical advances have been made available to mankind as an extension of His grace. Those are individual convictions and should be accepted with respect.

Regardless of our doctrinal position, however, it is important that we are *consistent* with our convictions. For example, many in the church have no problem taking medication for *physical* illnesses, yet they draw the line at taking medication for *mental* or *emotional* disorders. No matter how an illness is manifested, it is because something in the body (or brain) is not working properly, and medication can be used to help the individual *recover* or at least *cope*.

There are many types of antidepressants that have proven very helpful in the treatment of depression, and the newer ones have relatively few side effects. Normally, a physician can, in time, find the best medication and dosage that will enable the person to cope with life effectively. It is important to note that *antidepressants* are not the same as *tranquilizers* and are not physically habit-forming. (Generally, *tranquilizers* are given to mask the problem by helping the person feel better temporarily.) Antidepressant medication interacts with the chemicals in the brain (neurotransmitters) to enable the body to function on a more normal level.

The prognosis for recovery from clinical depression is very good. It may take some time for the medical practitioner to find and prescribe the right medication and dosage, as each individual case is different. As the person takes medication, finds emotional stability through support such as counseling, prayer, and the encouragement of friends and family, there is no reason why he or she cannot live a full and meaningful life.

Whatever we do, we must do in faith (Rom. 14:23). If we have no conviction against taking medication for a cold or the flu, then we should not be convicted (*or condemned*) for receiving medical treatment for anxiety or depression. At the same time, we can also hold to scriptural promises that God, should He choose, is able to heal *all* our diseases, whether or not we are taking medication.

Whose fault is it?

Another tactic that Satan used against me was planting the thought that perhaps it was the fault of others that I had not gotten better.

This is mindful of the man at the pool of Bethesda who complained that someone was always in his way (John 5). Sometimes Satan deceives us into believing if another person in our life would just straighten up, then surely, we wouldn't have so much difficulty. We might even think, "Well, I could get my breakthrough, if it weren't for dear brother so-and-so!" The sad fact is that the blame game can become an excuse for our non-acceptance of personal responsibility and lack of trust in God.

Sometimes, our greatest hindrances in life are not relationships, or any *one* traumatic event, but rather (what seems like) a *multitude* of ordinary aggravations—spoken of as *manifold temptations* in 1 Peter 1:6 (KJV)—that heap distress on the person and don't seem to let up. Satan uses a lot of lies to hold us back from believing God, but God's truth is there for people to grasp.

I wanted to develop my faith more than anything, but I first had to come to a place where I believed that God would help me, no matter what apparent hindrances or obstacles there seemed to be. In Isaiah 43:13, God says, "I will work and who shall hinder it or reverse it?" (AMP). That scripture indicates to me that there is absolutely *no one* or *anything* that can hinder God from performing His perfect will and purpose in the lives of those who trust in Him. Job said, "He performs [that which He has] planned for me, and of many such matters He is mindful" (Job 23:14, AMP).

The irony of all this was that God was using the very circumstances I hated in order to bring me to a place of total trust in Him. Sometimes God wants to change *us* more than our circumstances. When God does bring us to that place of surrender, we must be willing to say, "Okay, God... whatever!" God is looking for our cooperation and willingness to believe that He is leading and in control.

God's got me hedged in, and I can't get out!

I believe God allowed me to remain hemmed in by my circumstances that I might have the opportunity to learn that *faith* and *trust* are still the primary avenues which will lead us through the seemingly impossible obstacles in our lives. Jeremiah complained, "He hath hedged me about, that I cannot get out: He hath enclosed my ways" (Lam. 3:7–9 KJV).

The old-timers used to have a saying, "Shut up to faith." God, at times, closes all our escape routes so we are forced to simply *go through* certain situations. Surely, I wasn't the same person who had once sung, "Whatever it takes!" Surely not!

Charles E. Cowan wrote about being shut up to faith:

> God still shuts us up to faith (Gal. 3:23). Our natures, our circumstances, trials, disappointments, all serve to shut us up and keep us inward till we see

that the only way out is God's way of faith. Moses tried by self-effort, by personal influence, even by violence, to bring about the deliverance of his people. God had to shut him up forty years in the wilderness before he was prepared for God's work.

Paul and Silas were bidden of God to preach the Gospel in Europe. They landed and proceeded to Philippi. They were flogged, they were shut up in prison, and their feet were put fast in the stocks. They were shut up to faith. They trusted God. They sang praises to Him in the darkest hour, and God wrought deliverance and salvation.

John was banished to the Isle of Patmos. He was shut up to faith. Had he not been so shut up, he would never have seen such a glorious vision of God.[1]

Cowan goes on,

Are you in some great trouble? Have you had some great disappointment, have you met some sorrow, some unspeakable loss? Are you in a hard place? You are shut up to faith. Take your trouble the right way. Commit it to God; praise Him that He maketh all things work together for good, and God worketh for him that waits for Him. There will be blessings, help and revelations of God that will come to you that never could otherwise have come; and many besides yourself will receive great light and blessing because you were shut up to faith.[2]

Sometimes the only way out is "through."

As I repeatedly wore myself out fighting, I finally realized that I had been kicking against God's divine restraints. I had to learn to recognize the futility of trying to be in control of all my circumstances. I could not alter everything pertaining to my situation, no matter how much I struggled or kicked against what I did not like or understand.

I was slowly starting to get the message: there are going to be some experiences that we are just going to have to buckle down and walk through. Some of the "Red Seas" that we face may seem impassable. The "Egyptians" may seem to be hot on our heels. But we also realize going back where we came from is not the greatest idea either! God began to instill in me the necessity of going forward, no matter what I had to go through to do it. Through all my difficult experiences, God was teaching me to rely on His faithfulness while continuing to shape me to His will.

God is more interested in producing lifelong fruitfulness than an immediate deliverance.

At the time, God's methods seemed so harsh and uncaring. The scripture teaches us that although His dealings may at times seem *painful,* "afterward it yields the peaceable fruit of righteousness" (Heb. 12:11, NKJV). I have to be honest, though. There was a lot of that kicking nonsense still left, and believe me, God still had His work cut out for Him!

My keenly sensitive and observant husband was so kind to point out my one and only obvious defect (Did I say *one*?). He said, "Honey, you have a choice. You can kick and scream all the way through your depression, and probably, in time, you will come out of it okay. But you won't have profited any from it." He was right. Even though I might continue resisting like I was trying to win an "Olympic-style kicking event," it wasn't going to win me any medals, and it wouldn't change anything.

Missionary John Follette wrote:

> What are you seeking in your trouble today? Is it deliverance or development? You may have the one and not grow, or you may have both and grow. Take the positive attitude and use your trouble as one of

the most skillful and wonderful instruments God ever placed into your hands for the working out of the character of Christ to be duplicated in you.[3]

No repeat lessons please, Lord!

Many people do get over their depression or problems in time, but still may not have profited from the valuable lessons God wanted them to learn. God can only use the tool of trouble to mold us when we allow Him to. That is not to say that problems come for the sole purpose of teaching us something. *Trouble* is common in the life of all men, and while we don't pray for it, God can use our trouble as tools in which He not only manifests his purpose in our lives but to equip us for ministry as well.

Perhaps the greatest lesson learned is when we can simply say, "God, I really don't like this situation, but I'm going to choose to believe that You know something I don't know." Some of our revelations are really quite humorous, if you stop to think about them. Of course, He knows something that we don't know! *He's God!*

God wanted me to learn to trust Him, not only when I didn't understand, but also to trust Him to take a seemingly bad situation and reap something good from it. "All things work together for good" (Rom. 8:28, KJV) is either a truly inspired scripture or it isn't!

In Isaiah 48:17 (AMP), God announced to His people, "I am the Lord your God, Who teaches you to profit, Who leads you in the way that you should go." This scripture assured me that God wanted me to learn something in going through the experiences in my life. If no lesson is learned, how have we profited?

I did desire to find stability in my life, but I had the mistaken idea that I could only reach that place if things were perfect right now (at this very moment, please). And, of course, there shouldn't be any times of *testing* either. But much to my dismay, I found that scripture didn't agree with my expectations. It says in 1 Peter 5:10 that it is *after we have suffered a while* that God will perfect, establish, and settle us. So God is always working out His purpose in our lives, "For it is God that works in you both to will and do of His good purpose" (Phil. 2:13, NKJV).

Jesus is the storm stopper and the storm controller!

I'm reminded of the story in Luke 8:22 when Jesus stated to the disciples, "Let us go over to the other side of the lake." Then after making such a positive statement, Christ allowed a great storm to arise that threatened the disciples' very existence. Now since Jesus in His omniscience knew that the storm was going to take place, I wondered why He didn't just stay awake and do something to stop it in the first place. Have you ever felt that Jesus went to sleep on purpose? I'm convinced that God was up to something bigger than calming their storm.

He wanted them to learn that even though there was a storm going on around them that they would still be safe because He was with them. They should have realized if Jesus said, "We're going over to the other side" that nothing was going to stop them from getting there. The fact that they got so upset at Him was probably a good indicator that their belief system wasn't quite up to par. That might preach a good sermon! Our upsets might also be a good indicator of what we really believe.

I often have to remind myself that Jesus is always in my boat, even though He may appear to be responding in an uncaring manner. God wants to prove to us that no matter what storms may be raging, we can become steadfast and unmovable. Paul was able to write, "None of these things move me" (Acts 20:25) because God had already proven Himself faithful through previous storms.

It is unhealthy (as well as unrealistic) not to accept that there will be storms in our lives. The scripture plainly says (Isa. 43:2), *when* you walk through the fire—not *if* you walk through the fire. It also says, "Many are the afflictions of the righteous, but the Lord delivers him out of them all" (Ps. 34:19, NKJV). We live in a sin-cursed world, and as a result, at times, we will be affected negatively by its influence. It is through the storms that God proves to us His faithfulness to His Word!

You mean, I might not always be singing "Victory in Jesus"?

Another thing I hated about my affliction was that just about the time I started doing better, it seemed I would sink back down once more into depression. I learned that these cycles are not abnormal, but oh, how I grew to hate them! But did you know the Bible has something to say about "hills and valleys" in our lives? God told his people in Deuteronomy 11:11 that the land that they would be given to possess *is a land of hills and valleys.* In his book *Turning Mountains into Molehills,* Warren Wiersbe wrote about great people of the Bible who also faced their valley experiences:

> Abraham went through "the horror of a great darkness." Jacob wrestled all night until He was willing to surrender to God. David hid in a cave and wondered if the crown would ever be on his head. Isaiah lamented, "I have labored in vain; Moses cried out to God, "I am not able to bear all this people alone. Kill me, I pray thee." Isaiah lamented "I have labored in vain; I have spent my strength for nothing, I have spent my strength for nothing and in vain!" Then of course we see Paul in the New Testament as He cries out, "We were pressed out of measure, above

strength, insomuch that we despaired even of life." These men all knew what a valley was about."[4]

The Fear of Going Back

Most people have good days and bad days. Those recovering from depression may also go through significant *highs and lows*. (This is not to be confused with the extreme mood swings of Bipolar Disorder.) The down times may seem intensified due to the condition itself, and especially so, due to the constant fear that the sufferer might be slipping back into the depths of depression.

The person needs to be reassured (as often as needed) that during the recovery process, low times are to be expected, they are usually temporary, and that better times are ahead.

Sometimes we may be up. Sometimes we may be down!

It has usually been during the *valley time*s that I have learned (along with David) that God could offer me restoration for my soul and also give me some needed physical rest. I am still learning the need for balance in my life.

I recall reading about Corrie Ten Boom's "valley time" experience when she was forced into six months of bed rest.

She didn't understand why the debilitating circumstance was happening at the time, but she finally adapted by doing an in-depth study of the Bible and taking the unexpected time to seek God. It was years later when she realized that God had used that down time to prepare her for the ministry that was still in the future.

We can either fuss and fume or grow and bloom!

We may feel at times like God has shelved and forgotten about us. However, this unexpected down time can be a good opportunity for us to learn to go with the flow and utilize our time and circumstances with hope for the future. One author says:

> We argue with our Lord over his timing and fail to see that every day is a chance, full of purpose—even if we're waiting...So when your life is at a standstill over what you can't control, and when you're waiting on answers that never seem to come, God says to use that time to work where you are. God says to learn the art of waiting purposefully.[5]

This does not mean that we should never desire changes for the better or adopt a "well, I guess God is just putting me on the shelf, so I guess I may as well give up!" attitude.

However, if we are to learn effectively the art of coping, it will mean there may be times we will have to choose to find a way to be as productive as possible, regardless of the situation. I was hesitant about putting this idea into practice because I felt it might be saying to God that I didn't want anything to change, when deep down, of course, I did.

When we kick against our circumstances, the pain we feel is not so much from the problems themselves but from our resistance to God and His sovereignty.

During my intense struggle with depression, I have to confess there were times I felt I couldn't deal with my ordeal any longer. I had worn myself out more times than I'd like to admit as I *kicked against the pricks*. The only way out of my frustration was when I finally chose to begin living one day at a time. And often, it was *one moment* at a time. When we're really hurting, that is just about all we can believe for. Thank God, He has always been faithful to help me when I was willing to let go and *choose* to trust Him.

One of the ways God encouraged me to live *in the moment* is found in Isaiah 27:3 (NKJV):

> I the Lord keep it,
> I water it every moment;

Lest any hurt it,
I keep it night and day.

As long as my focus was on *me* trying to find solutions, I found I couldn't effectively handle life. But whenever I was able to bring Christ into the midst of my situation, I could find His peace, even though my problems were still there. I was slowly learning that God was my source of sustenance and safety.

Checking Up

- ✓ Many times, our first impulse is to run from situations that God has chosen to accomplish His will and purpose in our lives.
- ✓ When we struggle against our circumstances, it produces a discontentment that steals our joy of the moment.
- ✓ When we fight against God's will and purpose, we only end up frustrated and inflicting more pain.
- ✓ God has actually designed goads to prod us forward toward his goal and purpose for our lives.
- ✓ God desires a wholehearted surrender of our wills!
- ✓ God is more interested in changing *us* than He is in changing our circumstances.

- ✓ Many times, God allows us to be hemmed in by our circumstances so that we are shut up to faith.
- ✓ No one or nothing can stand in God's way and purpose, if we are yielded to Him.
- ✓ God knows things about our situation that we don't know or understand, and we must learn to trust His sovereignty.
- ✓ *Fussing and fuming* does nothing but hinder our spiritual growth.
- ✓ When we can't change our circumstances, we can focus on the fact that God is with us, no matter what comes our way.

5

THE AFFLICTION

I have chosen thee in the furnace of affliction.

—Isaiah 48:10 (KJV)

AFTER BEING HOSPITALIZED, my depression definitely improved, and I had been advised that I should continue on a prescribed maintenance dosage of antidepressant medication for at least a year after all symptoms had disappeared. But after many years of being depressed, I wanted desperately to be free from any connection with, or any reminders of, the disease. Somehow, I felt I could never truly be well as long as I was taking the medication.

I reasoned that if I quit taking my medicine, it would prove my faith to God. Now, if an individual is truly being led by God to do something like that, the leading will be confirmed by the *results*. In all honesty, however, in my case, it was not *God's* leading as much as it was my own desires to get off the medication—fueled by the pressures from others.

I soon found that my step of faith (which was really more of a stumble of presumption) only resulted in a further setback. It never dawned on me that God's concern was not whether or not I took medication; He just wanted me to trust Him to take care of my situation in His own way and time. One scripture that has become a great comfort to me is, "From eternity to eternity I am God. No one can snatch anyone out of my hand. No one can undo what I have done" (Isa. 43:13 NLT). God knows how to accomplish His purpose in our lives even when we don't!

Accepting God's sovereignty in our present adversity requires just as much a response of faith as it does to believe God for deliverance from it!

Isn't it interesting how many accounts of healing have occurred where God was not bound to any single method or action? It seems we are always trying to fit God into a neat little package or see His work accomplished according to an orderly set of principles. I will be the first to admit that I've been guilty of dictating how God is to do His job. But surprisingly, I found that just because Commander

Naaman had to dip in muddy water seven times (2 Kings 5), it doesn't mean that God requires everyone to take a dip before healing can take place.

I am convinced that a lot of the time we won't have the slightest idea of what God's plan includes or how He plans to accomplish it. We must continually seek for His direction, and if we don't feel God giving us specific guidance, then all we can do is wait on Him and leave our situation in His capable hands. I don't claim to be an authority on *healing*, but I have come to the conclusion that it pleases God when I can still have a trusting attitude, no matter what adversity I may face. I believe God will still fulfill His purposes in my life as long as I look to Him.

When all is said and done, there is no substitute for trust!

In one of her poems, missionary and writer Amy Carmichael wrote, "In acceptance lieth peace." I had to let go of my plan for my healing in exchange for God's plan before I could witness any kind of significant recovery. Ironically, it is often in humble acceptance that we are able to find a release from the anxieties that may be contributing to the adversity itself. This is not a fatalism that says, "Oh, well, what will be will be," either! Author Jerry Bridges said this:

We seek to escape from or resist the adversities, but all the while cling to the anxieties that they produce. The way to cast our anxieties on the Lord is through humbling ourselves under His sovereignty and then trusting Him in His wisdom and love.[1]

Who's in Charge Anyway?

To many Christians, *acceptance of their situation* is tantamount to *giving up their faith*. Some have been taught that acknowledging that they have a problem is a negative confession and will keep them from any hope of divine intervention. Others attach a spiritual logic to their situation by thinking, "If I admit to this problem/weakness and accept (earthly) help for it, I am *rejecting* what God may have in store."

There are several problems with these lines of thinking. First, it besmirches the nature of God. He loves us more than we could ever love Him, and He cares more about every aspect of our lives than our minds could ever fathom. Next, it puts the burden of what happens in the future upon us, rather than upon *the One Who holds the future*. It is not our thinking or behavior that determines what happens next; it is God Who is in control. Lastly, these ideas reflect a shallow and limited understanding of the biblical concept of *faith*. True faith is that which rests in God alone. When our faith rests upon our words, principles, doctrines, *or even certain scriptures,* which we have "claimed" for ourselves, we have ceased to have faith in God and have placed our faith in our concepts of faith or as some have put it, "Placed our faith in faith."

The three Hebrew children had that true faith as did Job, who fiercely held to his trust in the Almighty's will and purpose.

When I was unable to get immediate results, I slowly and reluctantly began to accept the fact that I did, indeed, have a chemical imbalance. *Depression!* How I hated the word! I felt like I needed to apologize every time I used the term to describe my condition. But then, Paul's *thorn in the flesh* (2 Cor. 12:7)—probably one of the most argued-about passages in the New Testament—became a source of help to me.

Evidently, Paul finally realized the only explanation He needed (or was going to *get!*) was the knowledge that God's grace would be sufficient for Him to bear up under the problem. Perhaps that also enabled him to handle any personal attacks or criticisms coming from his brethren. I decided if Paul didn't find it necessary to apologize or explain to everyone about his *thorn in the flesh,* then maybe I shouldn't have to either!

I had wanted God's help, but I had wanted it on my terms, and I really didn't think I could cope unless He resolved the situation my way. When God did not fall in line with my ideas, I had to realize that He was still a *very present help* in my time of need, and I just needed to let Him work it out His way.

Our need either drives us to God or away from Him.

So what could God possibly say to me that could give me encouragement for this special but ultrasensitive spiritual struggle in my life? The only thing I knew to do was to go once more to His Word where He had helped and given me reassurance at other times.

Before, when I had faced something too big for me to handle, God had always been faithful to speak to me from His Word. I knew from experience that God's Word could carry me through my storms. So as I frantically turned through the pages of my Bible, God faithfully began speaking to me once more, "Behold I refined you, but not as silver; I have tried and chosen you—in the furnace of affliction" (Isa. 48:10 AMP).

Somehow, in all my confusion, God illuminated those words to my weary heart. I read it again: I have CHOSEN YOU in the furnace of affliction. I knew God was speaking to me! Eagerly, I meditated on its meaning. God had given me a word of reassurance that He was with me, and having finally accepted that, I now wanted to know and find His purpose.

Chosen in a furnace! How comforting can that be?

I'm sure that many people wouldn't find the term *furnace of affliction* too comforting. Most of us aren't really looking for a furnace in which to suffer! But ironic as it may seem, those words did bring me comfort. It was exactly what I needed to hear because, like it or not, that's where I was! Even though I felt alone and forsaken, the Holy Spirit helped me to see that, in spite of my circumstances, God was still aware of where I was.

Through this verse, God was assuring me that He could somehow use this furnace to refine me and make me a vessel of honor for His glory. Because I continued to feel a lot of guilt and condemnation, this verse helped me to endure the most trying test of my entire life.

And thank God He knows how much we can stand. Arthur T. Pierson wrote:

> Our father, who seeks to perfect His saints in holiness, knows the value of the refiner's fire. It is with the most precious metals that the assayer takes the most pains, and subjects them to the hot fire, because

such fires melt the metal, and only the molten mass releases its alloy or takes perfectly its new form in the mold. The old refiner never leaves his crucible, but sits down by it, lest there should be one excessive degree of heat to mar the metal. But as soon as he skims from the surface the last of the dross, and sees his own face reflected, He puts out the fire.[2]

If we can't admit our need, it really is quite difficult to receive any comfort!

Paul wrote in 2 Corinthians 1:4 that God is able *to comfort us in ALL our tribulation.* One thing is certain: God can't comfort us if we don't let Him. I had to be willing to lay aside my self-sufficiency and image of grandeur I had erected of myself and admit that I needed help. The scripture says:

> Come to me, all you who labor and are heavy-laden and overburdened, and I will cause you to rest, [I will ease and relieve and refresh your souls.] Take my yoke upon you and learn of me, for I am gentle (meek) and humble (lowly) in heart, and you will find rest (relief and ease and refreshment and recreation and blessed quiet) for your souls. (Matt. 11:28 AMP)

I realized that even though this was a very uncomfortable furnace, God could use it to refine me and make me fruitful in His kingdom's work.

When we come to the place where we can begin to see purpose in what God allows, it enables us to have hope and keep on going. Perhaps you may be thinking that God can't possibly bring anything good out of your situation. One thing I have discovered about affliction is that God uses it to reveal many things about ourselves, and through our crisis experiences, He can always find something redemptive to teach us.

When God first shines His light on our weaknesses, it can be as overwhelming as when Paul was smitten to the ground (Acts 9:4–6). For a period of time, we may feel helpless because of what God's light reveals to us about ourselves. But He is faithful to remove the scales from our eyes so that we can become productive. As we discover who and what we are, we find strengths that we never knew we had.

It really doesn't matter whether I caused it, the devil caused it, or God just plain allowed it to happen!

I wondered if I were to blame for my condition. I carried a tremendous amount of guilt and condemnation, and often felt that the affliction was a direct result of my own failures and weaknesses. At other times, I felt that God (for whatever reason) had willed this to happen. And occasionally, I wrestled with the possibility that perhaps the devil alone was responsible—in order to attack my faith.

When we are confronted with any problem, it is never wrong to pray (as David did in Psalm 139:23–24, KJV), "Search me, O God, and know my heart…and see if there be any wicked way in me…." To be sure, I had failed God in the past, and if it had not have been for God's mercies, they would have bowed me hopelessly to the ground. But I was also reminded of the scripture that says, "For all have sinned, and come short of the glory of God" (Rom. 3:23, KJV). It is not that God overlooks our faults, but He is still merciful to us all.

And of course, the enemy of our soul is always present to bring his accusations and discouragements. When I would complain about his tactics, my husband would remind me, "That's what he does. That is why we must continue looking to Christ." Satan's nature is to discourage, and his intention is to wear out the saints (Dan. 7:25).

So in the final analysis, it really didn't matter whether I had caused my depression, the devil had caused it, or God had allowed it. He is still a redemptive God, and is in full control. "But though he cause grief, yet will he have compassion according to the multitude of his mercies, for he doth not afflict willingly nor grieve the children of men" (Lam. 3:32–33).

One author reminds us:

> God is in the restoration business, and He's more than willing to come when we call out to Him for help. Satan wants us to believe that God is sitting on His throne, huffing, "You got yourself into this mess; now get yourself out."[3]

Satan wants to destroy our lifeline called hope.

I wanted more than anything to please God, and for Him to work His plan in my life, but Satan continued to accuse me day and night for my shortcomings. I asked God to cleanse me and purify my heart's attitudes and desires, but never felt it was enough. A friend of mine (who also suffered from depression) expressed it so well to me: "Having depression made me feel so flawed."

There is a fragile brokenness that accompanies the unveiling of one's weaknesses, no matter what tool of trouble brings them to the surface. When I first began to see myself and my weaknesses, it was almost more than I could bear. I felt so sinful and worthless! Finally, I had to accept the fact that God didn't intend for me to die for my sins and weaknesses. Yes, I needed to be repentant, but God alone can carry the burden of sin and its penalty. All He asks of us is that we turn to Him "in all our afflictions."

> Surely He hath borne our griefs and carried our sor-
> rows…He was wounded for our transgressions, He
> was bruised for our iniquities; the chastisement for
> our peace was upon Him, and by His stripes we are
> healed. (Isa. 53:4–5, NKJV)

Reading Job 5:18, we find that the same hand that wounds is also the hand that heals! When affliction strikes us to the inner core and the pain becomes almost more than we can bear, it is then that our perspectives and goals in life slowly begin to change.

There is something about affliction that makes us more eternity conscious.

When God draws out His plans for our lives, He often shows us our weaknesses for the perfecting (growth and completion) of His purpose. First, I believe He makes us aware of the transience of this life as compared to eternity. Then He reveals to us how shortsighted and selfish our personal pursuits often are. As realization came, I knew I wanted more than ever before to please Him, and along with that new desire, I found my priorities and goals were beginning to change accordingly.

Of course, this new shift of priorities required that I now had to be willing for Him to restructure my life as I ventured out of my comfort zone. Forsaking the safe place that I had hidden in for so long was not easy. Yet I continued to feel God's goads as He gently nudged me forward. It was scary, but I remembered that Peter didn't walk on water until He was willing to get out of the boat!

I clung to Jeremiah 29:11 (NLT) where God said, "The plans I have for you...are good and not for disaster, to give you a future and a hope." I still doubted many times if it were even possible that God could have a good plan for me. But because I wanted it so much, I simply *chose* to believe.

When you need a lifeline to hang on to, it's surprising what the Holy Spirit will bring to your remembrance.

There were many who had tried to tell me, "Chris, one day, God will use this trial so that you can help others." At that time, I couldn't believe what they were saying. I didn't even get a goose-bumps confirmation. But I can tell you this: God brought their words of encouragement back to my mind many times. He proved His faithfulness to me as His plan continued to unfold. At times, it was actually turning into a somewhat exciting adventure, which gave me the impetus I needed to continue on. Even with a partial unveiling of His plan, however, the breaking process still continued with the Potter's hand ever upon the clay—me.

The breaking and molding were often more painful than the affliction itself!

It is not that God delights in the breaking process. He does nothing without purpose. "For our light affliction, which is but for a moment, is working for us a far more exceeding and eternal weight of glory" (2 Cor. 5:17, NKJV). In the beginning, I wasn't too committed to His plan, and so I had to pray repeatedly, "God, I'm willing for you to make me willing." It was so hard for me to stay focused on my commitment. It is often a great temptation to renege on our commitments when it starts to hurt a little. Perhaps this is what it means to bind the sacrifice with cords to the altar. Even though the breaking process was painful, I realized that God wanted to do a work in my life, and so it became easier for me to cooperate with Him.

During that time, God began dealing with us about following the doctor's advice to leave our pastorate. That involved yet one more altar commitment as we were challenged to submit our lives to God in order to walk down a completely new and unknown path.

At first, I went through quite a struggle, and then as usual, I decided I had it all figured out. I thought, *Well, if God is leading us in a different direction, it must be because He's going to heal me and free me from all my problems.* And so, with that kind of "I've got it all figured out" type commitment, I was willing to make the transition.

Just because we pray and accept God's will, it does not necessarily mean that everything will be smooth sailing from then on.

The transition turned out to be very difficult for us. We had to pull up our roots from a place where we had spent thirteen years of very fruitful ministry. Our older daughter had grown up there and was ready to start her senior year of high school. The change was very difficult for her as well.

I do, however, believe that discipleship sometimes includes breaking ties with people—and even with ministries—who are beloved to us. Jesus said, "Any of you who does not forsake (renounce, surrender claim to, give up, say good-bye to) all that he has cannot be my disciple" (Luke 14:33 AMP). I think many people remain unhappy and unfulfilled because they aren't willing to give up *all* (which includes the comfortable past and present) in order to follow Christ. Or if they do give it up, they keep looking back (like Lot's wife) to long after what they've had to give up! I heard one preacher say that Lot's wife turned into a pillar of salt because she was trying to quench her thirst with Sodom instead of God. So God made her a symbol of her own sin! (Salt usually leaves one thirsty.)

Transition can be opportunity for spiritual growth!

The doctors had advised us to leave the ministry. The most painful question on our hearts was, Why would God do this? Most of our life together had been in the ministry, and I thought if God really promised to use me, why in the world would He take us from everything we loved? It didn't make much sense. But as Paul said, "His ways (are) past finding out" (Rom. 11:33, KJV), and a popular song's lyrics says, "When you can't trace His hand, you can trust His heart."[4] Again, it seemed that everything around me was being shaken. But we had committed ourselves to God's leading, and there wasn't anything left to do but follow that path in spite of all the questions.

As we made our move, it seemed that my depression was taking a turn for the worse. The doctors had told me that moving was supposed to be something that would help me, but by the time we finally started getting settled in Texas, it seemed that the bottom literally fell out of everything. Our money was gone, and we had no income. It certainly appeared to me that God had made some terrible mistake. I'm reminded of the joke that says, "It's darkest just before it turns pitch-black." I certainly couldn't see how things could get any worse. Just when I thought the fire had surely finished its work in my life, it only seemed to be getting hotter!

The following (untitled) poem so well depicts what was transpiring in my life at this time.

> He sat by a fire of seven-fold heat,
> As he watched by the precious ore,
> And closer he bent with a turning gaze
> As He heated it more and more.
> He knew he had ore that could stand the test,
> And he wanted the finest gold
> To mold as a crown for the king to wear,
> Set with gems with a price untold.
> So, he laid our gold in the burning fire,
> Tho' we fey would have said Him "Nay,"
> And He watched the dross that we had not seen,
> And it melted and passed away.
> And the gold grew brighter and yet more bright,
> But our eyes were so filled with tears,
> We saw but the fire—not the Master's hand,
> And questioned with anxious fears.
> Yet our gold shown out with a richer glow
> As it mirrored a Form above,
> That bent o'er the fire, tho' unseen by us,
> With a look of ineffable love.
> Can we think that it pleases His loving heart
> To cause us a moment's pain?
> Ah, no! but He saw through the present cross

The bliss of eternal gain.
So he waited there with a watchful eye
With a love that is strong and sure,
And his gold did not suffer a bit more heat,
Than was needed to make it pure.[5]

Checking Up

- ✓ Faith can be defined in many ways; God is not necessarily bound to a specific type of response.
- ✓ Many times, all God desires from us is that we just accept His words of comfort and trust Him for the final outcome.
- ✓ God leads us individually, and quite often, we just do the best we can and trust Him.
- ✓ We may not always have the explanations we desire, but God's Word will always give us the comfort we need.
- ✓ God wants us to learn to admit our need so that we can receive His help.
- ✓ When we can see purpose in our problem, it helps us endure it.
- ✓ We will often go through a period of brokenness when God allows us to see our weaknesses.
- ✓ We must always believe that with God, we have hope and a future.

- ✓ Even when we are in God's will, it does not mean that the molding process will be pleasant or that things will always be smooth.
- ✓ Transitional periods can be opportunities for spiritual growth.

6

AT WIT'S END

They reel to and fro, and stagger like a drunken
man, and are at their wit's end. Then they cry unto
the LORD in their trouble, and he bringeth them
out of their distresses. He maketh the storm a
calm, so that the waves thereof are still.

—Psalm 107: 27–29 (KJV)

Closed Doors

THE MOVE HAD been exhausting for me both physically
and emotionally, and it seemed I had moved back to square
one with the depression. I thought surely I had finally
reached the bottom by now, and the only way to go was up,
but evidently, the bottom was further down than I thought.

I began to slip back into the numbed isolation I had
grown to fear. When I wasn't staring unfeelingly into space,

I was crying. We had heard of a Christian clinic in the area that helped people with emotional disorders, so we decided to contact them. My husband telephoned the clinic, and the representative encouraged us to come for an interview. I packed a small bag, hoping that receiving treatment in a Christian environment would straighten everything out. Our hopes soared as we made the hour's drive to the clinic.

The people at the clinic were very nice and attentive and assured us that they were ready to help, especially since we were ministers. We began to fill out the necessary papers, thinking God had surely led us to the safe haven for which we had prayed. Then one of the personnel called Jim to the front where they talked for several minutes. After a bit, my husband came back to where I sat. "They can't help us," he said. The problem was that our insurance only covered so much for emotional and mental disorders, and we had used almost all of it in the previous hospitalizations. The people at the clinic were very apologetic, but without insurance or cash, we were a poor risk.

As we drove out of the parking area, it was growing dark, and rain began falling on the windshield. It seemed to be a fitting end to a wasted day. I leaned against the passenger door, and with my head against the window, I began to cry softly.

Jim knew that going home was out of the question. He drove straight to Presbyterian Hospital's emergency room in Dallas. There, they quickly assessed the situation and arranged to have me taken into the psychiatric ward where I would spend the next several weeks.

We were penniless and jobless, and now, I was going to be hospitalized again for the third time. You talk about *manifold temptations*! As the door of my hospital room closed behind me that night, I felt more alone than ever before. I really wondered how God could be involved in all this.

God isolates us to reveal Himself.

Wanting the encouragement that only a mother and father could give, I desperately wished for their company. My dad was still having serious problems with his heart, so Mom was unable to leave him to come and be with me. I remember looking toward heaven and saying, "God, everyone seems to be deserting me. Why can't You send someone with the comfort I need?"

I clearly remember feeling that God was saying to me, "These circumstances are for your good." This isolation from my parents was all in God's timing and plan. It was becoming obvious to me that God knew that it was now time that I develop my own individual faith with Him. Thank God, when we are at wit's end, it does not mean that we are at faith's end. In fact, that's usually when faith really starts kicking in!

Frankly, I don't remember much about my third stay at the hospital. I had to undergo more ECT treatments; then, the renewed struggle over medication. I was also confused over the conflicting medical opinions of my doctors. The doctor in Tennessee had said a move would be a good change for me; but the doctor in Texas was saying that the move probably hadn't been a good idea! This became only one more frustrating question that I now had to deal with. But again, *wit's end* is not necessarily *faith's end*.

When knowledge no longer produces peace,
true relinquishment does!

Now I had a new lesson to learn. I knew I had prayed for God's guidance, but I couldn't understand why He was allowing so much confusion. Have you ever been in a situation where it seemed God didn't seem to be making His way as plain as He had promised? I'm sure Abraham wondered why God would give him a promised son, and then turn around and tell him to kill Isaac (Gen. 22). But even when God appears to be acting contrary to His nature, He still has a perfect master plan that will not violate His given Word. We just can't always see it! God didn't renege on His promise, and Abraham didn't have to kill the lad either.

In the midst of such crazy turmoil, I knew I had to continue to lean upon God. We all will undoubtedly face situations that are absolutely going to shake our confidence in earthly hopes, including people. I firmly believe God allows this in order that we might learn not to put our *confidence in the flesh*, and that means *our own understanding* as well (Phil. 3:3–4; Prov. 3:5).

Many times, I have been brought to the place where I have faced such stressful conflicts that I thought I couldn't make it. It's been at those painful points of struggle that I finally have had to relinquish the whole situation to Him to do as He chooses. But isn't that the whole point of total trust? Frankly, there will be times we don't have a desired explanation for things going on in our lives. That is where I've had to learn to say with the Apostle Paul, "For I know whom I have believed, and am persuaded that He is able to keep that which I've committed unto him against that day" (2 Tim. 1:12, KJV).

When the darkness closes in, survival depends on faith, not explanations!

I believe Job had a similar feeling (23:3) when he complained that He couldn't find God anywhere. I certainly identified with Job in his confusion. My own version might be something like, "I go forward, but He doesn't seem to be leading there, and I go backward, but He doesn't seem to be leading there. Like Job, I wondered, 'Where in the world are you, God?'" I felt like no matter what I tried, I couldn't find any evidence of God's guidance.

Slowly, I began to realize that God often allows things in our lives to come to such disarray that we will have to choose His promises just to *survive*. In fact, it is usually life's most severe trials that cause real faith to emerge. It is then that we learn that no matter which way the wind blows, we can be at peace with God through His Word alone. Of course, like most people, I would have preferred for everything in my situation to be a bit more *perfect*!

No matter how many twists and turns we go through, God is still faithful to get us to where we need to go.

After a few weeks' treatment and rest, I was released to go home. It seemed to me, however, that things would never be normal again.

I am so glad that God can work in spite of our (seemingly) feeble faith. He was still teaching me about His grace and mercy. He was showing me that even when I was overcome by personal weakness, He would still help me, as long as I kept looking to Him. Psalms 37:24 says, "Though He falls, he shall not utterly be cast down: for the Lord upholds him with his hand" (NKJV). We all will fall from time to time. And when we do, we need to know He's still there to help us up.

The loss of material things

As my need to *control* things was being stripped from me, God also began to strip away the security that I had in material possessions.

When we first moved back to Texas, we had placed our belongings in a storage unit. After living with first this relative and then another, my husband finally got a low-paying job at an electronics store, and our family moved into a small apartment. I remember asking, "How are we going to get my piano, organ, and all our furniture into this small apartment?" My husband went to the storage building to get our furniture, but soon returned with a rather disconcerted look on his face. The minute I looked at him I knew that something else had gone wrong. I was totally unprepared for the next bit of bad news.

He just looked at me and said, "Well, I have good news and bad news. The good news is—you won't have to worry about where you're going to put all your furniture. (He always has had a rather unusual sense of humor!) The bad news is—someone broke into the storage unit and took nearly everything."

Indeed, someone had stolen our piano, organ, beds, mattresses, chairs, TV, Jim's tools, and almost everything of value. The thief—or thieves—had cut our lock, stolen our stuff, and then put on another lock so it wouldn't be discovered. We had assumed that the storage units inside a locked fence were safe, but we were wrong. Our assumption that the units were insured was also wrong.

Looking back, it reminds me of the words of a song on the old *Hee Haw* TV show: "If it weren't for bad luck I'd have no luck at all. Gloom, despair, and agony on me!" Of course, I didn't laugh at our loss, but neither could I cry. It was as if I were completely drained from all feelings. Suddenly, those things just didn't matter anymore; I had nothing left to grieve over. We had lost our finances, our ministry, and now, our possessions. I wondered what else could possibly be left. I guess I should have been thankful that I didn't have Job's boils.

There is a song that says, "I lost it all to find everything." It's not that I was happy that I had lost so much, but God was teaching me that things are not what ultimately contribute to our happiness or fulfillment. Only Christ's presence and peace are the priceless possessions that make one's life complete. I can truthfully say that I felt God's power undergird and strengthen me beyond what I could have imagined possible. When we suffer the loss of earthly things, God will show us life's true treasures.

"I will give you treasures of darkness and hidden riches of secret places" (Isa. 45:3, NKJV).

God so graciously began to teach me about the things that contribute to real peace. My sister had begun sending me some teaching tapes, and I eagerly began to feed on the Word. As I encouraged my hurting spirit by God's Word, the losses that I had just experienced really didn't seem to matter anymore. I was finding that there are a lot of things more vital to living than material possessions.

Just when I thought the floods would drown me, God began to move in our seemingly hopeless situation. The Psalmist said, "You have set a boundary that they may not pass over" (Ps. 104:9, NKJV), and when God says it's enough, the downward spiral has to stop.

My two angels

Shortly after my hospitalization, I began receiving unexpected phone calls of encouragement and comfort. It was when I was at my one of my lowest points that God brought two wonderful ladies into my life. These two ladies, members of a church that we eventually started attending, came to me when I needed good godly counsel and encouragement. They not only became my friends, they were also women who showed great faith and compassion.

Prior to our move, my husband had been my primary faithful listener and counselor, but now, with his added work responsibilities (first at the electronics store and later as a staff member at a church), he was not able to spend as much time with me as in the past. So once more, God was faithful to supply the help I needed. But I don't for one moment believe that those ladies' presence in my life was mere happenstance!

The two wonderful women who God sent to me were actually an answer to my mother's prayers. She told me sometime later that upon learning of my hospitalization, she began crying out to God to send *angels*, if need be, to minister to me. It is so wonderful to know that God can send people to us who are sensitive to our needs.

God sent those angels into my life for nearly two years to encourage me, pray with me, and simply to be my friends. The reality of God's Word became apparent to me—"Are not the angels all ministering spirits (servants) sent out in the service [of God for the assistance] of those who are to inherit salvation?" (Heb. 1:14 AMP).

I will never forget the scriptures of encouragement they shared with me. One of the verses, found in Jeremiah 30:17 (KJV), says, "I will restore health unto thee, and I will heal thee of thy wounds." Up until that time, I had lost sight of a God who was still able to perform miracles. I had suffered for such a long time that I had nearly lost my ability to believe for anything. As I read that verse, I immediately sensed—for the first time in a long time—hope anew that God could still bring restoration and healing to the depressed person I had become.

Hope is an anchor to the soul.

When we are hurting, it is vital to keep alive our hope that God is still in control of our lives and is able to deal with our problems if and when He chooses. God will some-way and somehow find a way to give us the encouragement to sustain us in our times of need. Hebrews 4:16 (KJV) says, "Come boldly to the throne of grace, that we may obtain mercy and find grace to help in time of need."

We must be willing to admit our need and accept whatever helps He offers. If it means that we must accept a situation for the present, it does not mean we have to give up faith for a miracle. Concerning the supernatural, C. S. Lewis wrote, "Do not attempt to water Christianity down."[1] When we fail to include the supernatural in our theology, we steal the hope that God is able to do the impossible. The fact is, hope is an anchor that keeps us steady, and is important to maintaining our faith. Hebrews 11:1 (KJV) tells us, "FAITH is the substance of things HOPED for, the evidence of things not seen" (emphasis mine).

God can encourage us and meet our needs from unexpected sources.

It is so important to encourage the person in depression with continued words of hope. I remember receiving words of encouragement from a man I had never met. During one of my down cycles, I had been crying out to God (once more) for the strength to endure. Unexpectedly, I received a book in the mail from a person whom I didn't know. The book was entitled *Ever Increasing Faith* by Smith Wigglesworth. How I thank God that He knows when we need ministry, and it amazes me how He uses so many different ways to accomplish His purposes. I am absolutely convinced there are no happenstances with our God. "O the depth of the riches both of the wisdom and knowledge of God! How unsearchable are his judgments, and his ways past finding out!" (Rom. 11:33, KJV).

"And my God shall supply all your need…." (Phil. 4:19, NKJV)

Our finances were at rock-bottom. It seemed we owed everyone. I remember one specific occasion when we needed two hundred dollars right then. My niece came to visit one day and told us the Lord had spoken to her to give us some money. She gave us one hundred dollars, and I thanked her for it. But after she left, I remember thinking, "Isn't that strange? We really needed two hundred dollars." There came another knock at our front door, and it was my niece again—with another one hundred dollars bill in her hand. Almost apologetically, she told us that God had told her she hadn't given the right amount, and she was bringing us another hundred. God doesn't make mistakes with His math.

Then there was another miracle of sorts. Well, let me explain. An elderly acquaintance knew of our difficulties and offered us one thousand dollars during one of my hospitalizations. He told us that we could repay the loan whenever we became more financially secure and went on to say that in the event that anything happened to him, we would be absolved from any indebtedness. Now, I promise you we did not pray for the kind man to die, but he did.

But the biggest financial miracles had to do with the hospital bills. There was no earthly way that we could pay them. After our insurance maxed out, we still owed about four thousand dollars to the hospital in the city where we had lived. When my husband called them to make arrangements, he found that the hospital had been bought out by another medical group. That company had reorganized and wiped out all the debts owed to the previous owners.

We needed a doozy of a miracle!

But the real financial test was the amount owed to the hospital in Dallas. We simply did not have the several thousands of dollars needed to pay off that horrible debt. With no insurance to help, well, we really needed a miracle!

When I was ready to be discharged, Jim went down to the business office to get the clearance we needed to leave. He had no idea how we could ever pay such a huge amount. Even if we set up a monthly plan, we couldn't have made the first month's payment. The lady in the office looked over the several pages of bills and said, "We may have some grant money available for situations like this. Would you like to apply, just in case you qualify?" (Would a drowning man like to have a life preserver?)

A few days later, we received a letter from the hospital saying that the entire bill had been taken care of. You can believe it was a time to rejoice! After all was said and done, the only significant amount we owed was from the psychiatrist who had overseen my hospital treatment, and he allowed us to make manageable monthly payments until the bill was paid.

We often think of that night when we were turned away from the Christian clinic. We hadn't understood what was happening then, but God had everything under control. "Man plans his way, but the Lord directs his steps" (Prov. 16:9 AMP).

Once more, God was showing me that "His ways are not our ways" and that "His paths are in the sea and his footsteps are not known" (Ps. 77:19, KJV). Slowly, I was learning that I could trust him to lead me in the right direction, even though I might not always understand the detours.

God may seem to be late, but He always comes through!

And so, it was when things were absolutely beyond our ability to help ourselves that God intervened in marvelous, miraculous ways. He ministered not only to our needs, but to our weary spirits as well. I was learning that God would prove Himself, even at the midnight hour. It is when we face a *great need* that we can discover He is a *great* God!

Wit's End Corner

Are you standing at "Wit's End Corner,"
Christian, with troubled brow?
Are you thinking of what is before you,
And all you are bearing now?
Does all the world seem against you,
And you in the battle alone?
Remember—at "Wit's End corner,"
Is just where God's power is shown.

Are you standing at "Wit's End Corner,"
Blinded with wearying pain,
Feeling you cannot endure it,
You cannot bear the strain,
Bruised through the constant suffering,

Dizzy, and dazed, and numb?
Remember—at "Wit's End Corner"
Is where Jesus loves to come.
Are you standing at "Wit's End Corner"?
Your work before you spread,
All lying begun, unfinished,
And pressing on heart and head,
Longing for strength to do it,
Stretching out trembling hands?
Remember—at "Wit's End Corner"
The Burden-bearer stands.

Are you standing at "Wit's End Corner"?
Then you're just in the very spot
To learn the wondrous resources
Of Him who faileth not:
No doubt to a brighter pathway
Your footsteps will soon be moved,
But only at "Wit's End Corner"
Is the "God who is able" proved.[2]

Checking Up

✓ It is when we are in the storm and are at our wit's
end that we learn the importance of wholeheartedly
crying out to God.

- ✓ God will often allow us to be isolated from outside support in order to help us develop our own personal faith.
- ✓ There will be times when human understanding will fail, and nothing but simple trust in God will be sufficient to keep our minds at peace.
- ✓ At times, what God is doing in our lives may seem to conflict with our understanding of His Word.
- ✓ God's purpose during times of darkness is that we learn to walk by faith and not our feelings. This is where stability is born.
- ✓ It often takes the stripping of things before we find out what is really important.
- ✓ God knows how to set boundaries to our times of trials, and when He says it is enough, the storm will begin to subside.
- ✓ God's ways and resources are always much better than our own.

PART III

LEARNING TO ENDURE

His divine power has given to us all things that
pertain to life and godliness...

—2 Peter 1:3 (NKJV)

7

TRUST IS A CHOICE

What time I am afraid, I will trust in thee.

—Psalm 56:3 (KJV)

SOON AFTER OUR move and my third hospitalization, I was suddenly faced with a new and difficult challenge. Due to our dwindling finances, it had become necessary for me to take care of my four-year-old daughter. Ever since she was a baby, I had relied on the help of others for her care. Though God had helped me in many ways, my nerves were still quite bad.

I was learning that God's guidance often comes through the arrangement of our circumstances, but I was very hesitant about taking on another new responsibility. As a result of my husband finding employment, I now had the responsibility of the household, and that had been quite a challenge to my faith.

I was still very weak physically, and for the past several years had not been able to do housework. In addition to the chemical imbalance, I was already almost forty years old when my younger daughter was born. So if you think I cried out to God for help before (and I did!), you should have heard me get serious with Him at this point! I knew I had to have more faith, and I needed it in a hurry!

Faith, like a muscle, is strengthened through its use.

I wanted so much to regain my strength, but now to have the complete care of my daughter was really pushing me to my limits. After only a few days, I complained to my husband that I didn't see how I could possibly take on this new responsibility. I will never forget what he said to me. "Honey, we don't have any alternatives. Our money and insurance have run out. You've received all the medical treatment possible, so you're just going to have to believe God that He will help us with this." Jim wasn't being unkind to me; he just didn't know what else we could do.

I wasn't sure I even had *any* faith at that point because I thought if I had *real* faith, then I wouldn't be in such a mess. It was then that Romans 12:3 (NKJV) was illuminated to my mind: "God has dealt to each one the measure of faith."

There has to be a starting point for faith!

Again, the realization came: I would have to *choose* to believe, even though I didn't feel like I was capable. The devil had almost convinced me that I had thrown away all opportunities to operate in faith. The devil is a LIAR! (John 8:44). If he can't make you believe you don't have *any* faith, he will then tell you that you don't have *enough* to do any good! It is important to remember that even a mustard seed amount of faith is enough to remove a mountain and cast it into the sea (John 17:20).

Most often, though, our mountains don't always get cast into the sea at one whack. At least in my case, God did not come and give me a miracle of complete instant healing. Instead, He gave me the faith and confidence to believe for His help to do each task as it was put before me to do.

You see, there has to be a *starting point* for faith. Many times, God gives us faith while we're still taking steps toward either a mountain removal or a God-ordained purpose. A good illustration of a progressive miracle is found in the story of the ten lepers who came to Jesus in Luke 17:12–14 (AMP). The scripture says, "And as they *went*, they were cured and were cleansed." I began to do *in faith* what I had not been able to do in my own strength, and God continued to strengthen me to do more.

I do believe we should use our faith to believe for the miraculous, but regardless of the outcome of one's faith walk, our Heavenly Father is pleased when we just choose to believe Him no matter what. I finally chose to believe that even though God's deliverance was not instantaneous (as I desired), He would still sustain me and give me freedom in my furnace. That is what I refer to as *furnace faith*.

The three Hebrew children made a great declaration of faith when they said, "Our God whom we serve is able to deliver us from the burning fiery furnace, and He will deliver us from your hand, O king. But if not—we will not serve your gods" (Dan. 3:17, NKJV). Either way, they had made up their minds that they were not going to abandon their faith in an almighty and faithful God.

When faced with challenging circumstances, there is a tendency to draw back and make a protective shelter for ourselves. But the scripture tells us not only to live by faith but that if we choose to draw back, God is not pleased (Heb. 10:38). Even if I believed I couldn't change my situation by my little faith, God still required me to give Him the faith I had, in order for Him to work.

A mustard seed is pretty small!

It is said that a mustard seed is so small you can hold thousands of them in your hand. Do you remember the question God asked of Moses?

> So the Lord said to him, "What is that in your hand?"
> He said, "A rod."
> And He said, "Cast it on the ground. (Exod. 4:2–3, NKJV)

God never asks of us more than we are capable of giving. We always have whatever we need, in order to accomplish what He directs us to do. I believe God leads us individually, and I am not suggesting that He will lead everyone in the same manner. I do know we need to be willing to do whatever God directs us to do, even though, in the natural, it may seem like a step of futility or impossibility. Second Corinthians 1:9–10 (NKJV) says,

> Yes, we had the sentence of death in ourselves, that we should not trust in ourselves but in God who raises the dead, who delivered us from so great a death, and does[a] deliver us; in whom we trust that He will still deliver us...

It is not that God is not big enough for our problems; it is that we focus on the *size of our problems* instead of *Him*. Our faith can't grow as long as we're looking at the wrong object. We are to look continually to Jesus, *the author and finisher of our faith* (Heb. 12:2). Then we are no longer looking at the difficulty or trying to determine if our faith is enough.

God wants us to respond to His nudges!

I think a lot of us are willing to take a step of faith only after God first hits us over the head with a big two by four. It is great if some great miraculous sign appears in our sky, but it's not the way God usually works. As Elijah was waiting for God to reveal Himself, the scripture says,

> But the Lord was not in the wind: and after the wind an earthquake; but the Lord was not in the earthquake: and after the earthquake a fire; but the Lord was not in the fire: and after the fire a still small voice. (1 Kings 19:11, KJV)

Though God is certainly capable of giving some big spectacular manifestation of Himself, I believe generally, He speaks in that still small voice. We learn mature choices and responses through experience and discernment, which grow through having our senses exercised (Heb. 5:14, KJV).

As I continued to read God's Word, He was imparting strength to me to attempt to do things I had not previously been able to do.

We need to confront the giants in our lives.

When I made the commitment to *believe*, it did not come without great conflict. It reminds me of the butterfly that must struggle free from its cocoon in order to fly. My earlier responses had been to *run away* from the struggle. I have since seen countless, hurting people who seemed always to be looking for an escape route from their personal problems. Those responses are natural for us, as illustrated by King David's experience when he wrote:

> Fear and trembling have come upon me; horror and fright have overwhelmed me. And I say, Oh, that I had wings like a dove! I would fly away and be at rest…I would hasten to escape to find a shelter from the stormy wind and tempest. (Ps. 55:6, 8 AMP)

I had thought it would be easier to run from my crises than to have to confront them. The truth is, if we want to defeat our "Goliaths," we may have to get out of our "I want to play it safe" comfort zone. Due to all of the enemies who had come against me, my faith had almost become paralyzed. Now, however, God was encouraging me to use the weapons He had already given me.

More on the Fear of Going Back

In his first inaugural address, President Franklin Roosevelt addressed a national crisis by saying, "The only thing we have to fear is fear itself." That certainly applies to the person trying to deal with depression.

Even as clinically-depressed individuals begin to show signs of recovery, they may find "old symptoms" occasionally reminding them of the awful pit they were in. As those feelings overwhelm them, they wonder, "Am I going back?" It is very difficult, if not impossible at times, for the person to express faith in the face of what seems so real.

It usually takes some time for the individual to finally come to the place where he or she can rationally face those fears and say, "This is only a temporary feeling. It will pass and does not mean that I am returning to the depths of depression."

Sometimes all we know to do is to go to bed and get up!

One day, I received a phone call from my sister. That day, I was so discouraged that I started telling her all my woes and ended with, "I don't know if I have the strength to continue." I cannot count how many times I have said that! The pain I was experiencing from being stretched had succeeded in bringing me to a tremendous state of panic! I didn't know what to do.

My sister quoted a verse from Mark 4:26–27 (NKJV) which reads, "The kingdom of God is as if a man should scatter seed on the ground, and should sleep by night and rise by day, and the seed should sprout and grow, he himself does not know how."

I had become so mentally exhausted about everything; all I could do at the time was to go to bed and get up! Now you might think that is not a real great use of one's faith! However, the truth is that some days, we may not be able to soar like the eagles. Isaiah said (40:31, NKJV), "They shall run and not be weary." But he also said that (on some days), we shall *walk and not faint.*

Believe it or not, I was a track runner in my younger years and had acquired a reputation for jumping the gun at our track meets. So to *wait* or even to *walk* was not the state I preferred. But I discovered that when a verse of scripture became real to me, I had better camp on it! The instruction that I felt sure God was saying to me was I was to go to bed and get up! Now I realize that one-liner might not sell a million hard copies, but when it is what you feel God is telling you to do, it is probably the safest course of action to take at the time.

No matter how insignificant it may seem, if God says do it, it is important!

I do not claim to be the world's greatest *faith* teacher, but I have found there are many facets to that subject. About the time I think I have *faith* all figured out, I find there is another aspect I'm not too well versed on. If that discourages you like it did me, well, join my support group! But I can tell you this one thing: I'm learning that our lack does not make God incompetent. I believe God is willing to make up for our deficiencies, and I don't believe He labels persons unqualified to use their faith just because they don't have a theology degree and haven't already conquered every giant in sight.

In fact, if the truth were known, we all probably still have a few problems. But isn't that what faith is for? (We don't really *need* it when we don't have any problems.) God only asks us not to be afraid to use our faith.

When we are hanging onto God by a thread, we may become fearful that the thread won't hold us!

I began to claim the scripture, "What time I am afraid, I will trust in Thee" (Ps. 56:3, KJV). That may not sound like a great declaration of faith, but then, neither does "Lord, I believe: help thou mine unbelief" (Mark 9:24, KJV). God listens to what others might call a pretty imperfect prayer. I have found I don't have to have the right formula before God will help me because He is a God of mercy and compassion, and is faithful to meet us right where we are.

Can God get glory out of frog faith?

God used a lot of different things to encourage me to believe and trust Him. As I said, I never experienced great miraculous signs to prove God's care for me. He does know, however, how to get our attention with that still small voice.

Perhaps the silliest prayer request I ever voiced to the Lord was given just before my birthday. I had seen a silly-looking frog that was actually nothing more than a ceramic scouring pad container. I thought to myself how much I would like to have one. In addition to the frog, I wanted a burgundy flower arrangement. And then to add to my big list, I thought how nice it would be to have a big surprise birthday party. Now to fully understand this story, it is important to note that during this time, I was still so depressed that I hadn't even been out in public. So no one—not even my husband—knew about my secret wishes.

Well, my birthday came, and you can't imagine the thrill I received when God answered all three of my requests. I got the dumb-looking frog, the flower arrangement, and the surprise birthday party! God responded to my desires on a practical level where it really brought me a lot of encouragement. (And you thought God couldn't get any glory out of an ol' frog?)

It was during that time that my younger daughter had just turned five and was starting school. Even though I had resumed caring for her, I was still incapable of doing the necessary shopping required for her school needs. Also, Jim had taken a new administrative position at a church (another step of faith), and I needed to spruce up my wardrobe a little. However, I hadn't been able to do any of my own purchasing; I had not bought anything new for several years. I would go into a store and just stare, completely unable to focus or to make decisions.

But now, with my newly-acquired frog faith, I was finding it a little easier to ask God to supply my needs.

Frog faith really worked!

Shortly afterward, a lady from our church called and said she had some clothes she would like to give my daughter and me. In the box were clothes (size 6—just my daughters size) and also some clothes that were a perfect size for me. God even knew my dress size! (To be honest, though, I hope God keeps that size thing just between Him and me.) Those were wonderful answers to prayer that God used to let me know that He really does care and is concerned with our needs.

God has so many different ways of proving his love. "O the depth of the riches both of the wisdom and knowledge of God! How unsearchable are his judgments, and his ways past finding out" (Rom. 11:33, KJV). God proves Himself to us that we might have faith and trust in His goodness. It isn't that we will always get everything we ask for, but I believe He will give us that which is necessary to encourage us to persevere.

Don't ever let Satan steal your hope! Hope is your anchor!

I believe anyone suffering from an affliction has to maintain a hope in God's goodness. Hope is a predecessor to faith. Hebrews 11:1 (KJV) says, "Faith is the substance of things *hoped* for, the evidence of things not seen." I'm reminded of the story of Sarah and Abraham. The scripture tells (of Abraham), "Who against hope believed in hope, that He might become the father of many nations ..." (Rom. 4:18, KJV). The scripture says that Abraham kept hoping for God's goodness to come through for over twenty years. Now that's some kind of persistent hoping!

Just as God dealt with Abraham's faith for many years, I believe He may also deal with ours for what seems (to us) to be an eternity. However, since *He* is the *Author and fin-*

isher of faith (and not us) we might as well relax, and enjoy the trip!

God wants to encourage the faith of all believers.

My experience of discovering and practicing my faith has helped me not to be so quick in judging the level of another person's faith. It is so easy to stand on the sidelines and think, "Well, I certainly wouldn't ever respond that way!" We might even be quick to tell someone, "You just need more faith!" (Brother Job has *enough* comforters!) It's easy to criticize if we haven't had to struggle at times ourselves. One thing *testing* does for us is to make us more sensitive and compassionate.

Does Depression Affect Divine Guidance?

Discerning God's will is difficult at times, even for seasoned, mature Christians. It is doubly so for the person with clinical depression because depression and anxiety are usually intertwined. The victim's problems with concentration, exhaustion, and self-esteem merge to cause the individual to live in a perpetual state of hesitancy and doubt.

Depression robs people of their strength and confidence in virtually every area of life. It also affects their lives of faith. Feeling insecure in their faith walk, they may wonder about the validity of their salvation. When people around them draw attention to their lack of spiritual power, it does even more damage to their ability to feel in control.

As the person gains ground, he or she needs patience and encouragement from friends and family. There needs to be a daily reinforcement given so that in time, the person will again be strong enough to be sure of hearing God's voice and to act upon it.

I realized I had to start taking some responsibility for my thoughts and actions.

In the beginning, others had to make many of my decisions for me because I was so ill I just couldn't function. But as I began to improve, I realized that God now wanted me to step out into a new faith dimension and to choose to trust Him even if I should fall or make a mistake. After all, David said, "Though he fall, he shall not be utterly cast down, for the Lord upholds him with His hand" (Ps. 37:24, NKJV).

God began to motivate me to believe and trust Him by allowing a lot of challenging situations that demanded my getting out of the boat. God wanted me to learn that we can never find a safer support system than His unfailing Word. He did not want me to put trust in *my* own faith either since I had already discovered that my faith alone was never enough to see me through a crisis. I had to learn that it was primarily *His faithfulness to me* that was needed.

I was finding that when the storms came, they would often cause my fears to resurface, but I was also finding that when I cried out to God for help, He was always faithful to reach out to me.

Those initial faith steps were fueled by God, allowing me to be placed in a crucible of suffering where I knew I either had to grow or die.

In the midst of my suffering, God was teaching me not only how to respond to problems but also was reacquainting me with His faithfulness. Romans 5:3–5 (NKJV) teaches us this important truth:

> We glory in tribulations also; knowing that tribulation produces patience; and patience, experience; and character, hope. Now hope does not disappoint; because the love of God has been poured out in our hearts by the Holy Spirit who was given unto us.

God was teaching me an important truth: as we experienced His faithfulness in tribulation, we could then have faith and hope for the future. I was learning I could *choose to trust Him* always.

Checking Up

- ✓ In order for our faith to grow, it must be challenged by difficulties and opportunities.
- ✓ Satan will attempt to discourage us from using our faith in every way possible.
- ✓ We must learn to trust not in ourselves or even our faith but in God and His faithfulness.
- ✓ We don't have to be condemned about our level of faith because God is the *Author and Finisher* of our faith.
- ✓ We must learn to respond to God's little nudges.
- ✓ The pace of our race is not the most important thing. It is that we keep on running.
- ✓ Our personal struggles with faith help us to be sensitive toward others who are hurting.

8

HE TEACHES MY HANDS TO WAR AND MY FINGERS TO FIGHT!

Canaan is a place where we can learn to live victoriously, even with the enemy nipping at our heels!

IT IS TRUE that salvation is a gift, and we don't have to do anything to earn it. It is also true that in order to possess God's promises, we will find ourselves engaged in some real spiritual battles. The land of Canaan is not just *heaven* in the sweet by and by, but *God's land of promise* down here—where, although the enemy may be nipping at our heels, we can still learn that we don't have to lie down in defeat.

I wanted to possess my Canaan because I was tired of Satan's attempts to weaken and destroy my fruitfulness. I knew there was a *fight of faith* to be waged if I were to have any continued victory in my life. I also recognized that kind of victory was not to be predicated on my having a perfect set of circumstances. However, though I knew this was going to be a spiritual fight, I didn't just get up one day and decide that I was eagerly going to take on the devil and all his demons.

I do not believe we are to be overly demon or devil-conscious, but neither are we supposed to hide our heads in the sand and pretend Satan doesn't exist. God had to teach me a little balance from His Word. The scripture says, "Be sober, be vigilant, because your adversary the devil walks about like a roaring lion, seeking whom he may devour (1 Pet. 5:8, NKJV). The scripture says we are to "resist (him)... *in the faith*" (verse 9). Canaan is not a place that is conquered; it is a place of conquest. We will never come to the place where we have no battles, but we can come through our battles victoriously.

God's insulation

Early in my depression, I believe God insulated me for a period of time from the conflict that could have destroyed me—much like He did the children of Israel in the beginnings of their wilderness journey. For one thing, I was still so exhausted mentally and physically I didn't have the strength for a small skirmish, much less an all-out attack from Satan and all his cohorts.

But the time did come when I felt that God was instructing me to start confronting my giants. I was beginning to realize that my afflictions and problems would not exclude me from my responsibilities for spiritual growth.

To be sure, there were many voices still shouting their epithets of discouragement and defeat. There were (to name a few) the enemies of fear, indecision, unbelief, and perceived failure. I began praying and asking God to show me what I needed to do. One day, while reading the Bible, a specific scripture suddenly gripped my whole being. There it was in Psalm 144:1 (AMP): "He teaches my hands to war and my fingers to fight." I knew God was speaking to me through His Word and letting me know that He would equip me and show me how to do battle.

"I will go in the strength of the Lord God..." (Ps. 71:16, KJV)

I agreed with the Apostle Paul's words, "My strength is made perfect in weakness" (2 Cor. 12:9, NKJV), but I still struggled with the possibility that I might not have *enough* strength to survive even a little battle. However, I eventually began to understand that it is when we realize our own impotence that God's power and strength becomes available to us as never before. God also reminded me that I was not fighting the battle alone, "For the Lord your God is he that goes with you, to fight for you against your enemies, to save you" (Deut. 20:4 AMP).

I also began accepting that God had promised to empower me so I could no longer use my weakness as an excuse for unbelief. I meditated on the story of Sarah who "through faith…received strength" to birth the promise (Heb. 11:11, KJV). In the natural, she could not have conceived, but God changed the *natural* by Sara's acceptance and reception of the *supernatural*. Time after time, God revealed those kinds of scriptures to my heart, in order to build up and encourage my faith.

We step out; God brings the victory!

There have been many obstacles that could have hindered my progress and made me believe that Canaan was to be inherited by just a few near-perfect people. Isaiah 45:2 (KJV) is a scripture the Holy Spirit has so wonderfully quickened to my mind. It is a wonderful promise that simply says, "I will go before thee, and make the crooked places straight: I will break in pieces the gates of brass, and cut in sunder the bars of iron."

God was giving me all the encouragement I needed to step out and believe Him for victory. One does notice, I hope, that in order for God to go before us, we have to be *going* somewhere. He also began to show me how to be *armed* for the conflicts that I would undoubtedly face in the future. The first weapon with which I needed to arm myself was

The Knowledge of God's Word

> For the word of God is quick, and powerful, and sharper than any twoedged sword, piercing even to the dividing asunder of soul and spirit...
>
> —Hebrews 4:12 (KJV)

"I knew the weapons of my warfare were not going to be carnal, but mighty through God to the pulling down of strongholds" (2 Cor. 10:4–5, NKJV). I read what God had to say concerning the mind (verse 5). It speaks of His power for "casting down imaginations, and every high thing that exalts itself against the knowledge of God, bringing every thought into captivity to the obedience of Christ."

If the Apostle Paul Had to Do It, So Do We!

Paul's enemies in Corinth were a few (carnal) detractors whose minds were filled with doubt about his sincerity and who wanted to reason about his motives and reputation. The apostle, knowing he could never defend

---

himself with endless debate, elected to rely upon the Holy Spirit to override normal thinking processes with divine enlightenment. Satan brings his combative thoughts to us as well. He causes us to imagine all kinds of things in an attempt to block our fruitfulness. His thoughts implanted in our minds become fortresses too formidable to overcome unless we choose to accept *God's Word* as final, rather than our *logic* or *reason*.

> Whatever things are true, whatever things are honest, whatever things are just, whatever things are pure, whatever things are lovely, whatever things are of good report; if there is any virtue, and if there is anything praise worthy—meditate on these things. (Phil. 4:8, NKJV)

The Word was clearly giving me insight that I needed to renew my mind by cooperating with the Holy Spirit. This meant working to change a negative mind-set by saturating it with the Word of God. As I recognized the need to renew my mind, the Holy Spirit began to show me I had a choice in what I was to believe: was it going to be my feelings, my expert knowledge, or the inspired Word of God, which cannot lie? I accepted that my part was simply to obey the scripture and *have it renew my mind* (1 Cor. 2:16, Eph. 4:23).

I slowly began to see subtle changes in my thinking and responses. God had long ago given me His promise,

> So shall my word be that goes forth out of my mouth: it shall not return unto me void [without producing any effect, useless], but it shall accomplish that which I please and purpose, and it shall prosper in the thing for which I sent it. (Isa. 55:11, AMP)

Positive Thinking Alone Is Never Enough

There is a great difference between the (secular) concept of *positive thinking* and the (biblical) model of *mind renewal*. Even some in the church have tried to change their circumstances and/or behaviors by training themselves to think (and talk) in a positive way. While learning a positive attitude is certainly commendable, it still may fall short of God's plan for the believer. (Even a non-Christian can be positive!)

The biblical model of mind renewal involves saturating our minds with the Word of God as we are daily transformed by the Holy Spirit. As we meditate upon *His* revelatory thoughts, our minds are supernaturally transformed. We do not *try* to be positive; we *become* positive because *we have the mind of Christ* (as a result of the Spirit's transforming power). In 1 Corinthians 2, Paul spoke of the difference between the natural man and spiritual man as it concerns wisdom and knowledge.

Perhaps the key difference between *positive thinking* and *mind renewal* is that the former is often an attempt to *change one's circumstances*, while the latter emphasizes *changing the believer's attitude about the circumstances*. In Philippians 3 and 4, Paul wrote a great deal about the importance of *how we think*. Chapter four, verse eight sums up the formula for healthy thought patterns. (It is interesting that *cognitive behavioral therapy*—based on healthy thinking—has now become perhaps the primary treatment for *anxiety disorder* so many years after Paul's instructions.)

We must choose to make Christ Lord over our thoughts!

At first, my carnal flesh was screaming, "I can't do this, and why should I even be expected to try?" I was so afraid to relinquish control of my old mind-set and reliance on emotional *feelings*. I was finding that believing the Word can, at times, be a somewhat scary adventure when it is not the typical course of action one would normally take.

Of course, I am not suggesting that we are to act presumptuously and do something abnormal, just because we think that is more spiritual. That is the tactic Satan tried to use against Jesus (Luke 4:9). Satan tried to *push* Jesus into proving His position with God. Because the scripture seems to be paradoxical at times, I had to remind myself continually that I must always follow *the whole counsel of God* and not just a few select verses.

Even so, in those occasions when we know Christ has called us to walk on water, it still can be a bit challenging and uncomfortable to our flesh. (Just ask Peter!) Obedience and trust are the two necessary components of faith that become the active proof of our discipleship. Jesus himself "learned obedience through the things which He suffered" (Heb. 5:8, NKJV).

In the beginning, it seemed that every spiritual-warfare attempt was a step of utter futility. But I might suggest that there were probably a few onlookers who might have thought David's use of five little insignificant stones was a risky confrontation for an enormous enemy like Goliath. However, as one minister said, "A small stone in the hand of someone who believed God won freedom for an entire nation."[1] It is exciting to see how through the pages of God's Word and even yet today, God graciously multiplies man's efforts to meet the challenges more than adequately.

"The foundation of God standeth sure...." (2 Tim. 2:19, KJV)

I eagerly desired my mind to be renewed, so I somewhat feverishly began to read the Bible and every inspirational book or tape that I could get my hands on. I knew that it would be only through God's Word that my mind could be *renewed* and my thinking changed. Many of those resources did encourage and help me tremendously. I soon discovered the importance of remaining centered on the pure, unadulterated, and inspired Word of God as my primary source for true guidance and doctrine.

The Bible has to be our main reference point, or we can all too easily lose our moorings. Even good Christian books may have conflicting viewpoints on at least one biblical truth, and we can easily become confused if we are relying on man's interpretations alone. I have now learned to look for truths that are often repeated by real men and women of God, rather than some obscure point made by just one author.

I believe God's words to us are not hidden, and the Bible is designed to be understood easily by any seeking heart. It makes me a bit uncomfortable when any individual claims to have a deep revelation that no one else has ever been given. It should make any of us a little wary!

Just a word from my heart

Speaking of books and other sources, my desire is that others may benefit from what I share. However, I trust that no one would ever blindly follow my advice or instruction without first comparing it to what the Bible has to say. I don't believe that any information is valid if it in any way violates or contradicts biblical truth. The same warning, I believe, applies for counseling.

I believe counseling can be very helpful in the process of healing as long as it is a biblically-based counsel. I have learned, however, that even with the best of intentions, it is possible to counsel ourselves to death over some issues that are clearly and distinctly covered in the Bible. Any kind of assistance can be dangerous if we do not assimilate and apply the Word in our lives on a regular basis. In order for truth to bring "renewal and change," it must be incorporated into all of our thinking processes.

I believe that scripture is still the only unalterable and eternal truth that we have at our disposal. Matthew 24:35 (KJV) says, "Heaven and earth shall pass away, but my words shall not pass away." Why would we then even attempt to look for all our answers in man? People can fail, and methods can fail, but God can never fail. In fact, Galatians 1:8 (KJV) says, "But though we, or an angel from heaven, preach any other gospel unto you other than that which we have preached unto you, let him be accursed." Well, I could just stop and preach a little, but I've got to get on with this story and try to finish it before Jesus comes back!

"Jesus said, 'It is written,' and then He said, 'It is written' (again and again)!" (Matt. 4:1–10)

I can't emphasize enough the importance of the Word in my life. As a believer, I had a responsibility to use the Word (even as Jesus did) to defeat Satan. That meant reading the Word, rereading the Word, and again I say, reading the Word! The Word is a very powerful weapon, which as previously stated, is referred to in scripture as *the sword of the Spirit.*

As I began, childlike, to wield this sword of truth, I am sure I looked like a stunted sword fighter. Like any good fighter, I wanted to win a few victories, but I didn't seem to be having much success at this point. And that was the problem with my conception of my faith: my emphasis was still on the *I* part of it. Satan had deceived me into believing that even though I had Christ on my side, the battle was still largely up to me. This was bad news because I felt so unworthy and weak I couldn't assure myself of any real spiritual victory.

I was searching for some sort of self-worthiness, which I felt would qualify me to be an overcoming conqueror. This struggle finally brought me to one of the most important truths that I have ever learned: we do not gain victories because we have finally measured up to a certain sort of spiritual stature; we win victories because we recognize that Christ has bestowed upon us His power and righteousness, which enables us to be triumphant.

We must realize that it is *in Him, through Him, and because of Him* that we are ever able to overcome. The scripture says that God has "made us sit together in Heavenly places in Christ Jesus" (Eph. 2:6, KJV). It isn't because of *any* of our worthy efforts; it is *always* because of Him. What a simple but sure battle plan for success that is. Just as the old church hymnal reads:

> On Christ, the solid Rock, I stand;
> All other ground is sinking sand,
> All other ground is sinking sand.[2]

Then God began to teach me the importance of yet another weapon.

The Weapon of Praise

> Let everything that hath breath praise the Lord.
>
> —Psalm 150:6 (KJV)

Many have told of being set free from despair through *praise*. The most notable biblical examples might be Paul and Silas in the Philippian prison. Beaten and humiliated, with their feet in the stocks, they "prayed, and sang praises unto God" (Acts 16:25, KJV). The following verse tells us that those praises triggered an earthquake that opened the doors and loosed their chains, which eventually brought about their freedom. That is quite a testimony to the power of praise!

To be quite candid, in the darkest time of my depression, I couldn't even talk or think—much less praise. But I did manage to offer a few, almost incoherent prayers from somewhere in my spirit, and God mercifully heard my feeble cry.

As I improved and was able to grasp more meaning from the scripture, I began hesitantly to put into practice the weapon of praise. Of course, being the impatient one that I am, I had hoped my first utterance of praise would bring total victory to my situation. It did not happen that way. As one writer put it so well, "We are notorious for wanting a magical key to unlock every situation of life."[3]

Developing a lifestyle of praise

God did want me to praise, but more importantly, He wanted me to develop a *lifestyle* of praise. Perhaps that is one reason my victory did not come quickly because I might not have learned the importance and necessity of learning to give praise. I also learned that prison doors don't just bounce open because we've warbled our first little song!

There's more to praise than just being able to get a much-needed jailbreak! When we live in the *atmosphere of praise* while still in our prison, we are making a great impact on those around us who are watching our Christianity under pressure.

A Christian's praise—that disregards circumstances—is a powerful testimony to God's love, care, and faithfulness. Sometime ago, I found a scripture that supported this endeavor of living a God-honoring life:

> He who practices truth [does what is right] comes out into the Light: so that His works may be plainly shown to be what they are—wrought with God [divinely prompted, done with God's help, in dependence upon Him]. (John 3:21 AMP)

It's not that we are praising God *for* any bad circumstances that we may find ourselves in, but we are praising Him *in spite* of them. There is a song that I love that says it so well. Part of one verse reads,

> In the midst of it all,
> I shall stand and not fall,
> And, bless His name.[4]

Praise does lift our spirits!

In time, I discovered that praising God would lift my spirit and dispel the fiery torments against my mind. Psalms 8:2 (NLT) says, "You have taught children and nursing infants to give you praise. They silence your enemies who were seeking revenge." The KJV's rendering is that out of "the mouth" of (children), God is able to "still the enemy and the avenger."

Praise Is Always Pleasing to God

As the children were directing their praise to Christ in the temple, He was confronted by the chief priests and scribes (Matt. 21:12–17). Jesus met their displeasure by saying (alluding to Psalms 8:2, KJV), "Have ye never read, 'Out of the mouth of babes and sucklings thou has perfected praise?'"

Clearly, the message in both passages speaks of the need to be as a child (in contrast to depending on the knowledge and wisdom of the natural man) in order to receive God's gifts in simplicity of faith and, in return, offer complete, unpretentious praise that pleases Him.

We may also infer the dynamics of a supernatural chain of events: First, God has ordained that praise (to Him) and divinely imparted strength have a correlation. Next, when the enemy comes against us, we are to respond in the way that pleases God and opens the heavenly door. Finally, God responds to *our response* (of praise) by sending whatever is needed to help us overcome and/or endure.

Praise not only shuts Satan's mouth, but also leaves him dumbfounded. Many times in scripture God seemingly confounded the enemy in his tracks. Don't you know it just makes the devil hopping mad when he is doing his best to steal our faith, joy, and peace and we just turn our heads toward heaven and praise God? It wreaks havoc on his battle strategy. Arthur Wallis writes, "There are two weapons we must learn to use—joy and praise. They are the greatest morale-booster I know, and the enemy finds them thoroughly demoralizing."[5]

Scripture is replete with instances of victory wrought through the praises of God's people! Just look at what God did for King Jehoshaphat in 2 Chronicles 20:22 (KJV): "And when they began to sing and to praise, the Lord set ambushments against the children of Ammon...and they were smitten."

It is also important to note that praise ushers in the presence of God. I can tell you from experience that an awareness of God's presence is equally as important as any deliverance we might receive. *Praise* and *presence* are inseparable. The psalmist wrote, "But thou art Holy, O thou that inhabitest the praises of Israel" (22:3, KJV). It is clear that David hungered more for the *divine presence* than he did for deliverance as he cried, "Take not thy Holy Spirit from me" (Ps. 51:11, KJV).

During some of our difficulties, we may not have all the *good feelings* we would like. However, *feelings* are not to be confused with the truth of God's Word. God's presence may not always bring a "goose bump, exhilarating, knock to the ground" feeling, but I have learned that praise can bring a peaceful awareness that He is there.

Learning to walk by faith is learning to walk with or without tangible support. As one author writes:

> God knows just when to withhold from us any fixable sign of encouragement, and when to grant us such a sign...He wants us to realize that His Word, His promise of remembrance, is more substantial and dependable than any evidence of our senses.[6]

Speaking of living by our feelings

There have been many times that I have determinedly had to *choose* to offer the sacrifice of praise. I have always found it easy to praise God when good things were happening, but to offer Habakkuk praise was another matter. This great prophet of God declared,

> Even though the olive crop fails, and the fields lie empty and barren; even though the flocks die in the fields, and the cattle barns are empty, yet I will

rejoice in the Lord! I will be joyful in the God of my salvation. (Hab. 3:17 NLT)

Well, this was certainly a new kind of praise for me to employ.

This is the sacrificial worship that undoubtedly brings the most honor and glory to God. We *choose* to do it whether we're having a good day or not. Praising God in this way becomes a way of life for us, and it is a good way to help keep our faith strong. I like how one author put it:

> Anyone can praise when the conditions are conducive but it takes a mature believer to praise God when he is ready to come unglued. Discipline is required for the natural man to give over to the spiritual. Praise is the stepping-stone to preventing an accumulation of tension and weariness. Also, praise is the best way to break through fatigue of spirit. Our bodies need rest, but the body cannot really rest properly until the inner man is at peace.[7]

And we must not forget

The Weapon of Prayer

Praying always with all prayer and supplication…

—Ephesians 6:18 (KJV)

The Apostle Paul wrote that prayer is a necessary element of spiritual warfare. Jesus said to His disciples that "they should always pray and not to faint" (Luke 18:1 NIV). I can witness to the fact that a person who has struggled with depression is going to have a harder time with emotional constancy and endurance than most people. It is not easy to pray when, for lengthy periods of time, one doesn't have the slightest assurance that God is there.

Before my clinical depression, most of my real praying was done during times of personal crisis. At that time, I was definitely not a "first call" on the church's prayer chain. Surrounded by parents who really knew how to touch God, I was brought up knowing the importance of seeking Him, and I observed how continual seeking of God eventually brought results. I had been taught that diligent prayer was the only thing that would enable people to endure satanic attacks that might come against them.

So now, God was allowing me the opportunity to practice wielding this wonderful weapon in my own life. All of our other weaponry would be of little value if we could not draw the necessary strength to fight life's battles from our Heavenly Father. The scripture lets us know that even "young men will give up" if they do not "wait on the Lord" (Isa. 40:30–31 NLT), so you can imagine what might happen to a 'lil old lady like me! But did God say *wait*? Well, I don't much like the word *wait*! I really like *instant* victories! (Doesn't everybody?)

The best knowledge about prayer is found through practice!

A person can be full of knowledge without practicing its application. The scripture says in Hebrews 11:6 (KJV) that "(God) is a rewarder of them that diligently seek Him." I would like to add a thought here: so many times we think we are not praying effectively if we do not feel God or have an assurance that He has heard us. The verse does not say that He is rewarder of them who diligently *feel* Him. It says that He is a rewarder of them who diligently *seek* Him. Praise God! When you think about that fact, it might even make you start to feel a little something!

Prayer is about relationship and communion with our Heavenly Father. We may go to counselors to talk over our problems and never give a thought that our Father is eagerly waiting for us to come to Him. How that must sadden God. "Let us therefore come boldly unto the throne of grace, that we may obtain mercy, and find grace to help in time of need" (Heb. 4:16, KJV). I believe that means *every* time of need. Here are some of my own thoughts and experiences of prayer:

- As we pray, we are energized.
- As we pray, the powers of darkness and confusion dissipate.
- As we pray, we receive God's answers.
- As we pray, God helps us surrender our problems.
- As we pray, our hearts are cleansed.
- As we pray, we are strengthened.
- As we pray, we receive revelation supported by God's Word.
- As we pray, our spirits are set free from worry and anxiety.
- As we pray, we are given faith that no weapon formed against us can prosper.
- As we pray, our spirits are lifted.
- As we pray, the enemy has to flee.

There will be times we will not have the answers to life's complexities, and we will be so impotent in our own strength and knowledge that we will, of necessity, have to rely on the supernatural strength we can receive through prayer alone. It is usually when I have exhausted all other resources that I realize once more that it is "Not by might, nor by power, but by my spirit, saith the Lord of hosts" (Zech. 4:6, KJV).

And finally, there is the need for renewal of spirit, mind, and body, using

The Weapon of Rest

> There remaineth therefore a rest
> for the people of God.
>
> —Hebrews 4:9 (KJV)

God provided a time of rest—called the Sabbath—that was intended for man's well-being. Man was not designed to abuse His mind, body, and emotions continually, without allowing himself adequate rest and recuperation.

One of the areas that God has had to deal with me about is the balance between (His) ministry and (my) work. By nature, I tend to be a workaholic. I love the satisfaction and feeling of accomplishment of a job well done. But I am learning that if my activities make me an angry and irritable person, I just might not have things balanced quite right! Besides, if I'm mean and crabby, I'm really not sure how effective my ministry is going to be.

This requires a lot of diligence in the area of self-discipline. It has been said that structure and discipline are safeguards to a healthy lifestyle, but I certainly have had a few chinks in my armor on this one. I excused myself by thinking, "After all, isn't *discipline* just a little bit rigid and on the legalistic side? And doesn't God bless us with freedom from living under a restrictive set of rules?" Isn't it interesting how we try to convince ourselves of things using only the scriptures we prefer? One author gives this warning:

> The fact is, when liberty leads to license, you end up with a worse kind of slavery. It's great to step on the accelerator, but if you don't know how to apply the brake, you're heading for trouble!"[8]

Swinging from the chandeliers?

Many times, I have found myself working feverishly at a *high-adrenalin* speed, and I was having so much fun, it was exhilarating. I was swinging from the chandeliers, and I just wanted to go on swinging! Life, however, isn't meant to be lived on one continual *high*. Our bodies, minds, and emotions can't take it.

Recently, I have read numerous articles that confirm that millions of Americans are addicted to *adrenaline*. Since having to deal with depression, I have learned the need to discipline myself to relax at times. Occasionally, I still find myself getting too wound up, and I have learned to ask my husband to please tell me to sit down and cool it.

When we begin to give ourselves to ministry, it will cost us something.

"And Jesus, immediately knowing in himself that power had gone out of him, turned around in the crowd and said, 'Who touched my clothes?'" (Mark 5:30).

In the case of the woman who touched Christ's garment, Jesus knew that power had gone out of Him. I believe it was due to that loss of strength/power in ministry that Jesus sometimes withdrew from the multitudes because of the weariness He suffered. He needed time to refuel spiritually, mentally, emotionally, and physically because of the demands of ministry. He knew He could not continue day after day in ministry without rest for both body and spirit. Neither can we.

He maketh me to lie down, and sometimes, He maketh me to get up.

There still were many times when I wasn't able to ask for outside help. In those times, I simply breathed a prayer to God, asking him, "Please give me the space and opportunity to relax." God has never failed! David said, "He *maketh* me to lie down" (Ps. 23, KJV). God knows how to "maketh" me lie down! Someone has said that when a person has been stretched beyond what is reasonably healthy, he or she becomes much like elastic that has lost its resilience. It then becomes harder for the person to return to the original state of normalcy.

Again, I'm not talking about an extreme that would encourage a lazy lifestyle. Some folks might decide they need to give up all responsibility and get maid service too! Frankly, though, it seems that too many of us are living at a much too fast-paced speed and wearing ourselves out with busyness—busy with church, busy with kids, busy with grandkids, busy with jobs, busy with hobbies, and on and on. It is easy to fill our calendars so full that we don't have any room left for personal relaxation or waiting on God. Scripture confirms the necessity for times of quietness in our life. Isaiah 30:15 (KJV) says, "In returning and rest shall ye be saved; in quietness and in confidence shall be your strength." Even Jesus found it necessary to have quiet time (Matt. 14:23).

Work and ministry are an important part of life for me, but I am learning I cannot afford to become so oriented toward trying to meet the needs of others that I don't take time to get proper rest.

How can I know my limits?

I am aware of wonderful Christians who were great prayer warriors and were seemingly doing everything right. Yet during an unexpected turn of events, illness, or great crisis, they suffered a complete emotional breakdown. Though the medical community tells us that clinical depression does not *necessarily* result from any specific cause, many of those mentally and physically exhausted saints have admitted that they allowed themselves to become too busy in ministry without proper rest and relaxation. Some even acknowledged that they were trying to do the Lord's work in their own strength.

On the other hand, I know of people involved in Christian ministry who were placed in situations that demanded more physical and emotional strength than it seemed possible or reasonable to give. During those times, God seemingly gave a supernatural empowerment for their crisis times without any evident ill effects.

That may leave you wondering how in the world one can know what his or her personal boundaries are. I don't claim to be able to give you your answers, but I have learned that listening to God and making practical, common-sense applications have been equally important in balancing my own life. I'm still learning, and I haven't got it down pat yet!

I do not know the reason why one person may collapse under pressure while another remains strong; however, my purpose in sharing my thoughts is not to (necessarily) discover those reasons. Rather, my aim is to offer encouragement, communicate some general truths I have learned, and, hopefully, to point to the example of Jesus Himself.

Christ did, on many occasions, withdraw from the multitudes for rest and for refueling with the Father. I have tried to implement that in my own life. My mother once wrote down a little saying for me: "No vacations from Jesus. Who wants any?" Wouldn't all of us profit more from our times of relaxation and vacations if we spent a portion of that time with our Lord? When we don't, we usually come home feeling more worn out than before we went.

Burning out or rusting out?

We have all probably heard that old cliché that workaholics love to use, "I'd rather burn out than rust out!" As my husband mentioned in his comments in chapter 2, we don't have to do either. However, due to the fact that we are in an earthen vessel, we can make poor choices unless we continually look to Jesus for His direction and help.

As I said, I'm still learning and haven't come to a place where I know it all. One thing I have discovered is that when I begin to be overwhelmed and stressed and don't know what to do, the best course of action is to take time to offer up a silent prayer or find a prayer closet where I can pour out my heart to God and receive His help.

Paul told the believers at Philippi to "work out your own salvation with fear and trembling" (Phil. 2:12, NKJV). While he was speaking in a spiritual sense, I believe that principle can also be applied toward maintaining a healthy balance in our work, worship, and rest.

Learning to slow down and enjoy life is something I'm still learning to do. One of the most awesome truths about God's working all things together for my good (Rom. 8:28) is that as a result of my affliction, I have better learned to appreciate and enjoy the things in life that really matter. I have come to realize the importance of laughter, and that it is good to find something to laugh about even in the most serious situations. I have even learned that being able to laugh at myself occasionally can make living a whole lot more enjoyable.

Checking Up

- ✓ Canaan is not a conquered place; it's a place of continual conquest where we must face up to the giants in our lives.
- ✓ God deals with us according to how our spiritual lives are developing.

- ✓ God will equip us for our spiritual battles.
- ✓ We must—in cooperation with God—take steps of faith in order to defeat our enemies.
- ✓ As we assimilate and apply God's Word, it will produce results.
- ✓ Giving Christ lordship in our lives includes making him Lord over our thought life.
- ✓ Obedience and trust are two necessary components of our faith.
- ✓ The scripture must be our primary source of reference.
- ✓ Truth must be applied in order for renewal and change to occur.
- ✓ Spiritual battles are not won through our worthiness but because of *His* righteousness.
- ✓ We don't unlock prison doors just by one praise attempt; praise must be developed as a lifestyle.
- ✓ A sacrifice of praise should be practiced even when our life is coming apart at the seams.
- ✓ It is only through the Spirit's help that we are able to overcome life's difficulties.
- ✓ Work and ministry need the balance of personal worship, quietness, and rest.
- ✓ Even with acquired wisdom, we must continue to look to Jesus for His strength and guidance on a daily basis.

9

....

LIFE OUT OF DEATH

Finding a New Perspective

> My purpose is to give life in all its fullness.
>
> —John 10:10 NLT

I WANTED MY life back. Like most people who struggle with clinical depression, I had a keen awareness that I was merely going through the motions of living. Life's meaning and direction had been taken from me.

But I didn't just want life. I wanted *abundant* life. I desperately wanted to have the fruitful and joyful life Jesus talked about in John 15. That desire intensified within me as I was drawn to 2 Peter 1:3 (NKJV): "As His divine power has given to us all things that pertain to life and godliness, through the knowledge of him who called us to glory and virtue." That scripture seemed literally to jump off the page as I read it.

I already knew from experience that the *all things* that Christ promised was not speaking of personal possessions or material things. Real life is not measured by how much we own (Luke 12:15 NLT). I had personally discovered how easily possessions, position, and money could be stripped away. I also found that when a person is really hurting, *things* no longer matter all that much.

The divine exchange

All through my recovery, God's Spirit urged me to draw nearer to Him. Though I knew (mentally) that God offered all believers His *abundant life*, it seemed elusive to me. When I first accepted Christ as my personal Savior, He had filled such a big void and brought me His unspeakable peace. As a young, somewhat immature Christian, I thought my Christian walk would always be just as it had been in the beginning. I didn't realize that one's faith could be *tried* to the point that the person might not always have that salvation "feeling" that is often accepted as an authentication of our experience with God.

As stated in earlier chapters, it was some time later, as an adult, that God began drawing me to a deeper, more mature Christian walk. Though unaware that it was happening, I had allowed that *first love* experience to be taken for granted. Any spiritual growth was mediocre, at best. It was through the tremendous upheaval of my circumstances that God allowed me to see my great need to deepen my relationship with Him and grow according to His plan.

The Bible speaks of being changed into God's likeness (2 Cor. 3:18 KJV):

> But we all, with open face beholding as in a glass the glory of the Lord, are changed into the same image from glory to glory, even as by the Spirit of the Lord.

In order for that change to take place in our lives, the verse says that we are "with open (or, *unveiled*) face" to "behold his glory." This means that we must make a close inspection of what He represents—who the Word says that He is. As we continue to look unto Jesus and His Word, God's glory is reflected back to us, which brings about the change. It is interesting to note that as Moses continued in the presence of the Almighty that his face became so reflective of God's glory that he had to put a veil on his face (Exod. 34: 30–35). That kind of reflection is possible only for those willing to spend some time in His presence. Oh, how I desired that kind of manifestation to be present in my own life.

Years earlier, as a little girl, I would sit and watch my mother preach under the tremendous anointing of God and wish for that same glory to rest upon me. The depression brought even a greater desire than before as I now sought a deeper, more meaningful relationship with my Lord. Romans 12:1 (NLT) says,

> My dear brothers and sisters, I plead with you to give your bodies to God. Let them be a living and holy sacrifice—the kind he will accept. When you think of what he has done for you, is this too much to ask?

I sensed that the Holy Spirit was asking me if I were willing to surrender myself more fully. At first, I thought surely God wouldn't ask me to submit the little life I was finally experiencing (or regaining) as an offering back to Him. Then I realized, isn't that what sacrifice is all about? It's about being willing to give up something that is precious or valuable to us. Would any of us really want to give an offering to the Lord that "costs us nothing" (2 Sam. 24:24)?

God had dealt with me on many previous occasions, but I had only made a lot of partial commitments. But a partial surrender really isn't surrender at all. Thank God, He was so patient as He waited until I was willing to make that commitment to Him.

One reason I hesitated making a full surrender was because I was afraid of what a yielded life might entail. I thought, "If I really yield to God it'll kill me, it'll finish me off." Not bad insight! Do you suppose that might have been the original intent of the scripture? I honestly didn't think I had enough spiritual tenacity to carry a cross at that point. I even considered the possibility that God wouldn't expect such discipleship from a person in my condition.

The fact is, God did want my flesh to be crucified!

> I have been crucified with Christ. It is no longer
> I who live, but Christ who lives in me.
>
> —Galatians 2:20 (ESV)

It didn't take too much to set me off. I had blamed so much on my affliction. My erratic emotions had made me quite vulnerable and a bit too sensitive. A better word might be *touchy*, but of course, that never applies to one's *own* persona! After all, I had a good *excuse*: I was suffering with *depression*!

At first, the demands of the crucified life exceeded my somewhat frail and "already stretched to the max" faith. I concluded that my affliction should excuse me from such an exacting commitment to God, especially since I was so weak and fragile. But there it was in Colossians 3:5,

"Mortify your members" (put to death the habits and attitudes in your life that are not like Christ's). Well, I didn't even like the word *mortify*! It sounded so cruel, insensitive, and *final*, and I didn't want any part of it! I even reasoned that since God is referred to as a loving God, surely He wouldn't want me to suffer any more than I was already. Living a crucified life certainly seemed a little too uncomfortable to me!

Why Would a Loving God Allow...?

The question is asked over and over, and with endless variations:

- Why would a loving God allow little children to starve?
- Why would a loving God allow good people to suffer pain and cruelty?
- Why would a loving God allow war and strife to continue?
- Why would a loving God allow my life to be turned upside down?

Sometimes the questions are asked by enemies of Christianity who are attempting to use human logic to argue that there is no God. (If there were a God, surely He would bring *good* in the place of whatever is *bad*.) Sometimes, similar questions are asked by Christians out of personal confusion, anger, or frustration. For the atheist who has no spiritual desire or discernment, there can be no satisfactory answer. And even the believer, when overwhelmed by human feelings and emotions, can become insensitive to spiritual truth.

Frankly, we are always at a disadvantage when we try to explain the *whys* of God. We see so little of the picture and only from our (limited) perspective. It would be comforting to be able to stand in the place of the Almighty Creator and always be able to say with certainty, "This is why God has done this or allowed that, but we cannot. There are, however, some things that God has shared with us in His Word that will help us when confusion, and doubt would crowd in upon our faith and trust.

First, we must remember that God did not bring evil into His perfect world. After Creation, He pronounced it "very good" (Gen. 1:31). The Father determined that humanity would not be puppets or robots but would be given *choice* in determining how to order their lives. It was only after Satan's temptation and man's disobedience that sin, with its resulting pain and sorrow, entered the picture. One day, there will be a new earth recreated to perfection (Rev. 21). In the meantime, everything and everyone on this planet has been affected in some way by the scourge of sin. God is not the author of evil; Satan bears the blame for human suffering.

Jeremiah learned another important lesson about the relationship between God and suffering (Lam. 3:32–33). Even in the times when God allows grief to come, his mercies will be available to compensate for the pain. Our loving God does not willingly afflict or grieve his children (verse 33), and we have a High Priest who shares every pain we bear (Heb. 4:15).

Hebrews 11 reminds us of faithful believers of all times who have kept the faith in the face of personal tribulation. They all knew pain and suffering, and many gave up everything—even paying the ultimate price—for their service to Christ. They all accepted the comfort of their Savior in the time of trial, looking with joy toward their future eternal reward. Many see them depicted as the "great cloud of witnesses" (Heb. 12:1, KJV) and as models for our own race on this earth.

We must not be trapped into blaming God for human heartache and misfortune. Rather, we should find comfort in knowing that He is always available to us as a help in time of trouble (Ps. 46:1).

Taking Up the Cross

I wondered what it really meant to "take up my cross" and follow after Christ. I now believe that to live the crucified life means that I no longer demand my so-called rights, but rather, I seek to please Him. That includes following after Christ regardless of the cost. Jesus set an example for us: "For I do always those things that please [the Father]" (John 8:29, AMP). Then two verses later, He said, "If you abide in my Word [hold fast to My teachings and live in accordance with them], you are truly my disciples."

This was a scary adventure for me. I knew the Holy Spirit really had His work cut out, and if I started giving up even a few of my rights, where would it all end? I know everyone is probably dying to know what He started dealing with me about, so I will tell just a little. I think down deep, we all like that "skeleton out of the closet" stuff! But seriously, I believe we all encounter struggles that threaten to defeat us, and I trust that my honesty will be an encouragement for others to know that most of us really do struggle with God on pretty much the same level.

The Stuff in the Closet

First of all, I was not nearly as submissive a wife as the Proverbs 31 lady. I would really like to know where she came from, anyhow! (Just kidding, of course.) She seemed so absolutely flawless, and I certainly fell quite a bit short of her unbelievably perfect image.

Then there was the thing with my temper. Of course, you must understand that I came from a long line of Germans, so I had every right in the world to have a temper! But as God began to deal with me, I knew I couldn't continue to blame my lack of restraint on my seemingly hotheaded ancestors. I haven't as yet found any scripture that supports the excuse, "I can't help it; I was born that way, and I just can't change my personality." But the scripture *does* say, "Is there anything too hard for God?" (Gen. 18:14, KJV).

God's dealing with me about my temper has resulted in a few pretty embarrassing experiences. On more than one occasion, I've had to return to sales clerks and apologize for my less than sweet behavior. Just because we don't think someone knows who we are doesn't mean we're not supposed to be good witnesses. (Just thought I'd throw that comment in for us "Goody Two-Shoes" who act like such saints on Sunday morning around the church folk.)

There have also been those numerous times when, because of my own struggles, I have lashed out at those I loved the most. How often are we prone to do that? It has been said that hurting people hurt people, but I couldn't find a scripture reference to excuse me for that one either! It's quite interesting how we try to rewrite the scripture, isn't it? Actually, God may call us to suffer in silence and shed our tears in secret. Jesus showed us by His own responses how we are to live:

> When He was reviled and insulted, He did not revile or offer insult in return; [when] He was abused and suffered, He made no threats [of vengeance]; but He trusted [Himself and everything] to Him Who judges fairly. (1 Pet. 2:23 AMP)

Our discipleship should be a result of allegiance, not compulsion.

We are to bear our cross even as Christ bore His, and we are to bear it out of the same love and obedience to God that He showed. It is when we finally come to that same purity of response that true discipleship is born. While it is true that Christ suffered and died that I might live, I also have to acknowledge Christ's words that say "The disciple is not above his master" (Matt. 10:24, KJV), and "Whoever does not bear his cross and come after me cannot be my disciple" (Luke 14:27, NKJV). God truly convicted me, and one thing I have learned is when that occurs, it is definitely the right time to start cooperating.

Up until then, God had given me a time-out season where He had seemingly allowed me to make a somewhat partial commitment. But now, it was time for a little more pruning as He began showing me the cost of true commitment to His Lordship. Ravi Zacharias writes:

> Hardly anyone likes the word "discipline." It is both the blessing and the bane (cause of harm) in our lives. Discipline always seems like a weight around our necks. But if one can only see the need for and the fruit of discipline, one can understand why it offers such great rewards.[1]

Down deep, I knew God wasn't trying to be mean; He simply wanted to bring me into a more fruitful and meaningful relationship with Him.

God's plan may at first seem difficult, but God says, "For I know the plans I have for you, declares the Lord, plans to prosper you and not to harm you, plans to give you hope and a future" (Jer. 29:11, NIV).

God does know how to bring us to the place where we will want to cooperate with Him. Philippians 2:13 (NLT) says, "For God is working in you, giving you the desire to obey Him and the power to do what pleases him." God had finally brought me to a place where I wanted to comply with His will.

I recently ran across a great thought:

> All of life may be divided into two parts: the first mile of compulsion, and the second mile of consecration. In the first mile, one is constantly demanding his rights; on the second mile, one is looking for opportunities. The mile of compulsion is a burden; the mile of consecration is a great joy.[2]

When God directs us to move on and commit our all, we need to obey so we will not miss the opportunities and blessings that He has planned. I call this His "stirring the nest syndrome." However, I believe God does give us seasons where we are more comfortable than at other seasons. And I am thankful for those seasonal rest breaks, because...

Just when you think you're almost perfect, God will come and prune you a little more!

So the seasons for pruning continue, and usually at those times, I struggle anew as once more, the Holy Spirit demands a more complete surrender. I have always wanted to be a vessel that God can use for His glory and a channel through which He could work, but I have learned that there will be an ongoing fleshly struggle in which I will have to engage myself in order to be molded more and more into His likeness.

Part of this pruning often includes a separation from the wrong motives that so easily can creep in and affect pure discipleship. In my case, I have had to address the question of whether my striving to follow Christ is out of undefiled love and obedience or because reason tells me if my discipleship becomes acceptable enough, I might be rewarded with complete healing. I never voiced those words aloud, but deep in my subconscious mind, there was a struggle going on that constantly demanded some sort of reassurance that God would be fair with me. I wondered if God would reward me and resolve all my pain if I truly gave Him my all.

How Good Is Good Enough?

It was stated earlier that the person struggling with depression often grasps at straws. His or her mind says, "There's a secret that you have missed." The individual is very susceptible to anything that promises relief and may begin to analyze all (outward) circumstances and (inward) thoughts and behaviors with only one main thought in mind, *Will this help me get well?*

The Christian may look at spiritual things through that same analytic filter: "Maybe I became depressed because I didn't pray enough, read my Bible enough, involve myself in ministry enough." Once blame for the problem is attached to a lack of discipleship, the next step is to correct it by (over)compensating.

The person may think, "If I can be the Christian I should be, all this will go away." He or she doesn't realize that they have fallen into the works trap, and no matter how good a Christian he or she might become, it will never be enough. It is at that point that passion and zeal can turn into a fanaticism that is actually counterproductive because it keeps the individual from resting in and relying on the grace and mercy of Christ.

God does not play "let's make a deal"!

I believe if we all were completely honest, most of us have at times been guilty of such bargaining. You might wonder (as I did), "What does it really mean when He says His plans are good and not evil and that He will reward us for following Him?" We usually think of a reward that includes things we may desire such as the solving of a problem or the healing of a body or relationship. Let me make it clear; these things are not bad to desire or believe for because God does care about every aspect of our lives. However, I do believe that the desired place that God wants to hold in our lives is our Heavenly Father, with no strings attached.

> There is only one kind of life that pleases God. There is only one kind of life, which really knows victory. That is God's life. Our life can never be filled with God's life until we let Him put our life to death every day. It is only as we choose to let Him be Lord that we can ever enjoy His life.[3]

A Chosen Vessel Fit for the Master's Use

One really can't call Jesus *Lord* if the person constantly wants to negotiate deals and call all the shots. I had to learn that there is more to discipleship than just receiving personal blessings. To be a disciple, one must be willing to be taught and led. It has been said, "If He is not your Lord, He cannot be your Teacher." If we want to grow in our relationship with Christ, we must give Him the right to correct, reprove, and prune us as necessary. Just ask me. I am a pruned example!

I don't know why we struggle so about giving Christ His deserved position, when deep in our hearts, we really do want God's help and direction for our lives. Satan tries to discourage us from full commitment because (1) he knows that God's plan is the only one that brings true fulfillment, and (2) it is through submission to God that we become fruitful and productive. So Satan tries to preoccupy our minds with selfish motives and wrong desires.

In order to follow Christ fully, we must be willing to take upon ourselves *the nature of a servant* even as Christ did (Phil. 2:5–7). This kind of a response of love and obedience will never demand something in return. Ravi Zacharias says, "There is no way for the will to be empowered to do God's will until it first dies to its own desires and the Holy Spirit brings a fresh power within."[4]

To be a chosen vessel means that we must keep our lives continually yielded to Christ. That means that we must allow Him to change us in whatever way He deems necessary.

He teaches me to profit (getting some new perspectives)

I believe that truth is revealed as we are willing for error to be dispelled. When we tenaciously hang onto our own ideas, we usually don't give God much room to work. As Christ began to change my thinking, I slowly began looking at things from a different viewpoint than I had in the past. I no longer felt the need to protect my great intellect; I simply wanted to learn.

One of the scriptures that God used to reassure me of His help is found in Isaiah 48:17 (NLT). "I am the Lord your God, who teaches you what is good and leads you along the paths you should follow." What a beautiful thought that has been to me—to know that God would be my teacher and my shepherd as well.

One of the ways God had been able to impart spiritual truth to me was through adversity itself. As one author put it, "A crisis can clear your perceptions as you behold His face, looking for answers that will not be found in the confines of the situation."⁵ Personally, I believe it is often through crisis that our ears become more finely tuned to His voice and our mental perceptions are sharpened.

Do I really love God for who He is or for what He does?

Job's whole trial hinged on this statement Satan made to God:

> You have always put a wall of protection around him and his home and his property. You have made him prosper in everything he does. Look how rich he is! But reach out and take away everything he has, and he will surely curse you to your face! (Job 1:10–11 NLT)

So I was faced with a difficult question. Would I wholeheartedly serve God even if I didn't get anything in return? Job must have considered that possibility when He said, "Though He slay me yet will I trust Him" (13:15, NKJV). The disciples were asked by Jesus, "Are you also going to leave?" (John 6:67, NLT). In the following verse, Peter replied, "Lord, to whom would we go? You have the words that give eternal life" (NLT).

By now I knew from personal experience that Christ was and is the very essence of life and living. I knew I couldn't and didn't even want to try to make it on my own. We really are not our own anyway (1 Cor. 6:19–20). As E. Stanley Jones said, "We simply hand back to God the self that is handed to us."[6] Truly it is only in Him that we can "live and move and have our being" (Acts 17:28, NKJV).

You can be mastered by your circumstances, or you can—with God's help—master your circumstances.

As I continued to study God's Word, I came to believe that I did not have to be *victimized* by my circumstances. I didn't know how God could change my thinking, but I wanted to believe He could. In the beginning, my old mind-set did not change easily, but I found my thoughts being adjusted as I continued to open up more and more to the truth of the Bible.

By this time in my spiritual journey, I had finally eradicated the notion that Christians were immune from having problems. All I had to do was look around and see that there were many others besides myself who were also suffering. Life's trials can be packaged in troubles such as the loss of a loved one, a broken relationship, an illness, a divorce—and the list go on.

One of the interesting things that God was showing me was that problems were really not the main problem in my life. It was how I was responding to my problems. A prime example of a godly response is from the Apostle Paul as he wrote (concerning his bonds and afflictions), "None of these things move me" (Acts 20:24, KJV).

God had already proven to me that He would be with me during the storms that came, but I still needed to let go of the reins of my life and begin to trust Him completely.

Wither and die, or relinquish and live!

When I demanded that my objectives be met instead of choosing to relinquish them to God, those plans always seemed to wither and die. But as I realized that God had a perspective on things that I could never have, I was able to accept that He could be trusted to take full responsibility. That enabled me to be free and to retain His abundant life, regardless of the circumstances.

The three Hebrew children were just as free from bondage *in* the fire as they were *out* of it. The scripture says they *walked around in the fire*. In order to profit from my affliction, I needed to see it no longer as an imprisonment. In the books of *Ephesians* and *Philemon*, the Apostle Paul referred to himself as "a prisoner of Jesus Christ." I believe he was saying, "Satan, you can't put me in bondage. Even in chains, I'm still free because I have the Greater One living on the inside of me." He also believed that God was greater than his problem and could deliver him whenever and however He chose.

When we really want to know Christ, our losses and our crosses no longer matter!

To effect a change will carry a price tag. When we become willing to allow the self to be crucified with its passions, lusts, and wants, it often is a painful death. One popular minister writes:

> The shaping of a will...requires a visit to the garden of Gethsemane. Gethsemane literally means "oil press." God presses the oil of his anointing out of your life through adversity.[7]

If we're willing, God will bring us to that place of anointing.

I knew that God wanted to fill me with His fruit, but until the spirit of *self control* was completely broken, God's fruit could not be seen clearly in my life.

Afraid of exposure

Then came the next pruning—God began to deal with me about my relentless desire for man's approval. Throughout my life, I had experienced the heartache and stress that comes from trying to be liked and admired. I wanted people to understand me and think that I was perfect. (A bit of a grandiose idea, huh?)

Even though I had improved physically to the point that most people would never have known about the clinical depression or spiritual battles I had fought, I was still afraid of my weaknesses being exposed. I was so concerned that others would be disappointed in me or think I was spiritually flawed.

Pride and insecurity can be horrible diseases that eat away at a person's very core. I have had to bring all of my weaknesses to Him and lay them on the altar. I know that it is important to know ourselves, but I have learned that I don't have to continue seeking the rest of my life, trying to find reasons and excuses for why I am like I am. In my quest for personal insight, I have come to the conclusion that God alone really knows me. The scripture says we don't even know ourselves (Jer. 17:9), but I believe God has a way of letting us know *what we need to know*, and then He gives us the power to change what He wants to be changed.

People will not always know or accurately discern our spiritual struggles, but regardless of whether we're always understood, we still don't have to be overly concerned about what others think of us. I do believe that we have to be accountable to our brothers and sisters, but I also believe our greatest sensitivity must always be reserved for God and not the approval of people.

Seeking a new kind of approval

When I finally grew tired of secluding myself in order to prevent public failure, I asked God to help me break free from the need I had for people approval. That was not easy. By now, there had been plenty of people who had judged my clinical depression and found me a little bit spiritually wanting! I really couldn't blame them, but it still fried my pride. To be misunderstood completely and misjudged by others just wasn't one of my favorite pastimes! Actually, they may have been partly right in their judgment, but I am so glad that God is the One who accurately sees the whole picture.

He also knew I didn't want to remain in bondage to what I felt people thought about me. One day, as I was reading the Psalms, God began to birth a desire for a new kind of people approval within my spirit. The tears begin to flow down my face as I read, "Even when I am old and gray, do not forsake me, O God, till I declare your power to the next generation, your might to all who are to come" (Ps. 71:18, NIV).

Now I had a new prayer. It wasn't for me to be exalted for any of her accomplishments, but rather, I now wanted to be a testimony of God's power, grace, and mercy. My prayer simply became, "God, please let my life be a witness to those I love. Don't let my life be in vain, and (as I had prayed in the beginning), Lord, whatever it takes, please make me like you.

It is God Who establishes, settles us, and makes us complete!

I realize that *suffering* is not a twenty-first-century theologically correct word, but the scripture does say (1 Pet. 5:10 AMP):

> And after you have suffered a little while, the God of all grace [Who imparts all blessing and favor], Who has called you to His [own] eternal glory in Christ Jesus, will Himself complete and make you what you ought to be, establish and ground you securely, and strengthen, and settle you.

This lets me know that in the end, any suffering I endure will be worth it. Again, in Psalm 131:2 (NKJV), we are told that there is a peaceable result obtained when we cooperate with God to become more spiritually mature. It says, "Surely I have calmed and quieted my soul, like a weaned child with his mother; like a weaned child *is* my soul within me."

The mask I had always worn was slowly being removed, and I was learning how to be more transparent. I was also accepting that it is not unrealistic for any accomplishment to include falling, getting back up, falling again, and then having to get back up again and again. That can be an embarrassment, but with God's help, it's the only way to keep on going. Another scripture offered me encouragement by letting me know that a righteous man (or woman) may fall seven times but will get up again (Prov. 24:16). I was tired of being nonexistent and hiding from the world. I wanted to live, and if it meant I had to risk making myself vulnerable, so be it.

One author states, "There is a season of establishing, settling and testing, during which we must "stay put" until the new relationship gets so fixed as to become a permanent habit."[8] In my case, I found it necessary to stay the course until the changes that God wanted to make in me had a chance to become a new and permanent way of life. As disagreeable as *suffering* might be, it is often necessary in order to make us into what God wants us to be.

It's not what we have to lose; it's about the life we have to gain.

The *eternal* perspective I have saved until last, and yet, it is perhaps the most important one of all. The reward of the cross is that through death, new life can be brought forth. Alice Flowers, a matriarch of the faith, expressed it this way:

> No seed ever springs into new life until it has fully died, become dead indeed…We may then face the overthrow of some cherished plan for God, the thwarting of some objective. But if we will but hold

on out of this seeming wreckage, God will build a better thing of richer design. And someday we will say, "Behold what God hath wrought."[9]

What a wonderful example we have of Jesus, Who through death was renewed and resurrected so that He would have the power to change and bring life to others. The scripture promises us that if we are willing to "purge (ourselves) from (the works of the flesh), (we) shall be a vessel unto honour, sanctified, and meet for the master's use, and prepared unto every good work." (2 Tim. 2:21, KJV). It is only when we allow God to strike a blow to our *self* (which includes the fleshly cravings and desires we think will make our lives enjoyable) that we can discover the *true life* that Jesus gives in exchange.

One may wonder if such a life is even attainable. I'm not talking about sinless perfection because I had tried all my life (in vain) to accomplish that. But neither am I implying that we should live our lives any way we please, just because we've been given liberty! Paul reminds us, "Do not use liberty as an opportunity for the flesh" (Gal. 5:13, NKJV). What I am talking about is simply agreeing—"Yes, I am willing to die in order that Christ might live in and through me." And He will certainly receive all the glory because, as Paul said in another place, "The life which I now live in the flesh I live by the faith of the Son of God, who loved me, and gave himself for me" (Gal. 2:20, KJV).

I must accept responsibility for my own responses!

There are valid hurts in all of our lives that need God's healing touch, but I had to be willing to see that there are also attitudes and actions in my life for which I am responsible.

In today's society, we are allowed to blame our situations on just about anyone or anything. If we don't do that, then we can blame it on some deep hidden agenda or repressed memory. Part of living the crucified life is that we will be held accountable for our responses, and we can't blame them on our circumstances, the devil, or other people. It is surprising how much we can stay on a merry-go-round, chasing down all the excuses that we can find in order to rationalize our behavior.

I believe that even when people do find reasons for their undesirable behaviors, they often don't find the cure. If there are those issues of unresolved hurts, unforgiveness, or bitterness, we still must turn to God for the remedy. Only He can supply the grace and power needed to resolve most of those issues.

When we feel that life has been unfair, we not only have *to choose* to forgive those who have hurt us, we must *choose not to blame God* as well. If we fail to do the latter, we will begin to distrust Him and form a God concept that is bitter and unjust. To place our continued trust in Him is not always easy, but it is still necessary for receiving overcoming power in our lives. We have to remind ourselves that God always knows something about our situation that we don't know. He is God; therefore, we won't be able to understand all of His ways, which are "past finding out!" (Rom. 11:33, KJV).

Looking to the Past or Looking toward the Future?

In Christian circles, there are differing opinions about the fields of *psychology* and *counseling*. One extreme says that psychology is based on secular principles and has no place in Christianity. Therefore, to those in that crowd, any counseling that utilizes psychological principles is a tool of the devil. The other extreme makes room for all kinds of foolish, unscriptural practices that are made to appear Christian by spiritualizing the terms used or taking scripture out of context.

Psychological thought, as a study of human behavior, has actually been around since pre-Christian times. There is nothing inherently wrong in trying to figure out why humans think and act as they do. And there is nothing wrong in seeking Christian counsel during times of doubt, discouragement, or depression. There are some things, however, that should be kept in mind.

First, probing into the past can be a lifelong and futile pursuit. Freud, who gave birth to *psychotherapy*, said no one can be cured of their neuroses; there must be a continued addressing of past issues. Those who look to find hidden memories are also dredging up yesterday's muck that may (or may not!) have happened. Many families have been torn apart by counseling that brought things to light that probably never occurred.)

Secondly, we should acknowledge that *most* of the things that affect our thinking and behavior are not really that difficult to pin down. Sometimes, undetected physiological problems complicate matters, but for the most part, our dilemmas are relatively easy to figure out. Somehow (we think), if we can mystify our past, we can absolve ourselves from any needed responsible responses in the present. It can be very convenient and somewhat entertaining to poke around in our history, analyze our dreams, or investigate the symbolism of our actions. On the other hand, it isn't so enjoyable to apply the light of scripture to our lives. However, the Bible still outranks any psychological manual when it comes to explaining human behavior or determining what is right and wrong.

A competent Christian counselor will gently, but firmly, point to God's Word as the final authority for all human responses to life.

Lastly, we should look to Christ as our counselor/model. He never berated anyone who came to Him for past misbehaviors. He didn't make people soak in condemnation before they could receive His touch. He never required penance to purchase hope for the future. "Go and sin no more" (John 8:11, KJV) was both admonition and encouragement. In the Bible, an encounter with Jesus meant that new life began from that point on, and Christian counseling should always include an encounter with Jesus.

Life stinks when we deny God's sovereignty over people and situations!

Hebrews 12:15 (NIV) says, "See to it that no one misses the grace of God and that no bitter root grows up to cause trouble and defile many." When we think that life stinks, we are inadvertently implying that God isn't being fair with us. Paul didn't make such a selfish choice; He rejoiced in saying, "I count all things but loss for the excellency of the knowledge of Christ Jesus my Lord: for whom I have suffered the loss of all things, and do count them but dung, that I may win Christ" (Phil. 3:8, KJV).

We too can live the crucified life by faith in the redemptive work of Christ, which has paid the price for us to walk in newness of life. My dear father penned a simple but beautiful poem about his desire to walk with Christ above all else. He was a wonderful, generous, and kind minister who constantly showed the beauty of God's life working through him to others.

Eternity

> Help me, dear Lord, to live for Thee
> In the pure light of eternity—
> Counting all earthly gain but loss,
> Glorying only in the Cross.
>
> All my own goodness I disown,
> Only to live for Thy praise alone.
> Help me, dear Lord, to live for Thee
> In the pure light of eternity.

—Rev. F. R. McAdams

Checking Up

- ✓ God not only promises us abundant life, He also knows how to create within us a hunger to have it.
- ✓ God is good to show us that true riches are found only in Him.
- ✓ It is often through great upheaval of our circumstances that a renewed thirst for God is created.
- ✓ The crucified life includes giving up our "rights."
- ✓ We must stop looking for excuses in order for God to work His changes within our natures.
- ✓ Our motives for following Christ are changed as we continue to walk and yield to His workings in our life.
- ✓ God will continue to prune and convict us so that we may be more fruitful.
- ✓ True surrender does not hinge on our manipulation or bargaining.
- ✓ Pure discipleship is birthed as our motives are purified and our love for Christ increases.
- ✓ Our response to life's difficulties will determine whether or not we become victims.
- • To establish and settle us, all God asks is our cooperation.

PART IV

FRUITFULNESS

It is while we yet clench in our hands the
broken fragments of our life that God asks
us to give back to Him the tear-stained
remains that He might use them as healing
agents to soothe and comfort others.

10

·····················

FRUITFUL IN THE
LAND OF AFFLICTION

For God has caused me to be fruitful
in the land of my affliction.

—Genesis 41:52 (NKJV)

AS I SLOWLY continued my recovery, I began looking
around for ways I could be less focused on my own needs.
God began to birth in me a great desire to reach out to
others who were hurting. It is God Who works within us,
conforming us to His purpose by placing His desires into
our lives. One day, while reading the story about Joseph, I
ran across the verse "For God has caused me to be fruitful
in the land of my affliction" (Gen. 41:52, NKJV). As I read
it, I couldn't help being struck with the fact that Joseph

had become fruitful in a land where He had undergone intense pressure. Here was a young man who not only had been sold into slavery but also—through the false accusation of Potiphar's wife—was unjustly thrown into prison (Gen. 39).

I think I would have been tempted to sit down and nurse my wounds a bit. But instead, Joseph continued to be productive, and whatever his hand found to do, he did with excellence (Gen. 39:22). The part that really caught my attention was how Joseph responded to the butler and the baker who had subsequently been thrown into prison for offending the king.

The scripture says that Joseph ministered to their physical needs by serving them (40:4). Then verse 6 says that one morning, Joseph noticed their countenance and asked them why they were so sad and depressed. As they opened up to Joseph and told him about their dreams, he was able to minister to them in a spiritual way. It was plain to see that this was a young man who had learned to look outside himself and his own problems in order to minister to the needs of others.

Later (even more surprisingly), he offered to interpret a dream for the king (chapter 41). This is particularly interesting to me because if anyone ever had a reason for not cooperating in giving dream interpretations, Joseph was that man. Don't you know the devil was probably mocking

Joseph about his own dreams? I can almost hear Satan say, "And you call yourself a dream interpreter! Ha! You couldn't be too great at interpreting dreams. Look at your own dreams and what's become of them!" But instead of Joseph becoming disillusioned and bitter, he allowed God to make him fruitful, even while enduring His own affliction.

I think I might have wanted to tell my prison acquaintances a little of my own story of injustices. But instead, Joseph compassionately reached out and ministered however he could. Interestingly enough, God must have been pleased with his response because the scripture goes on to say that God made Joseph to prosper in all that he did. Joseph must have probably got an *A* on his *dying to self* report card!

A famous evangelistic team also passed that same course with flying colors. After being unjustly arrested, the jailer threw them into the inner prison and placed their feet in stocks (Acts 16). After Paul and Silas led a midnight praise-and-worship service, God's applause shook the place and set all the prisoners free. But when the fearful jailer would have taken his own life, Paul stopped him, and he and Silas ministered to him and led his whole family to Christ.

This was a difficult concept for me to follow. I was so consumed by my own pain it was hard for me to look outside myself. But I knew God was encouraging me at least to give it a try.

Then came the accusations!

I wanted so much for God to use me, but Satan was whispering in my ear, "Who in the world would ever listen to you?"

I thought, *There's no way I can have any sphere of influence for the kingdom in my condition. Just look at me!* I was still somewhat dependent upon others myself. So why did I even think I was qualified enough to help someone else?

I knew the Bible said that God "comforts us in all our tribulation that we may be able to comfort those who are in any trouble, with the comfort with which we ourselves are comforted by God" (2 Cor. 1:4, NKJV). However, even though God had been faithful to help me many times, I still had a tendency to limit what I could do for Him. Thank God, in spite of my reluctance, He allowed my nest to be stirred to the point that I figured I might as well cooperate.

Our weaknesses should never be an excuse for not allowing God an opportunity to prove Himself to us.

Though I was willing to be used, I was still consumed with my own limitations and how much I should risk extending myself to others. I was growing older too. It's natural to think we can do less as our bodies start to decline and become more fragile. Yet I could not cloister myself from the needs of others. Every time I began to turn inward to become lost in my own needs, I would think of some servant of God who refused to allow *self* to stand in the way of *ministry*.

Even now, I think of my precious mother in her mid-eighties, who still had a zest for life and a word of encouragement for everyone she met. She and my dad (who died several years ago) were people of faith, and they lived it! On meeting my mother, one might think she was problem-free and had never had any trials. Well, as one ol' gal used to say, "Honey, you don't know nuthin!" She had been through the fire many, many times. Until her recent passing, though no longer involved in full-time ministry, she continued to witness, encourage, and win the lost. And if you think she was going to let *me* give up, you've got another thought coming! It was hard to give in to self-pity with her on the sidelines cheering me on!

As we minister to others, God ministers to us!

One day, as I was reading from Isaiah 58 (NKJV), I ran across a precious passage of scripture that says (verses 6–7):

> Is not this the fast that I have chosen: to loose the bonds of wickedness, to undo the heavy burdens, to let the oppressed go free, and that you break every yoke? Is it not to share your bread with the hungry, and that you bring to your house the poor who are

cast out; when you see the naked, that you cover him; and not hide yourself from your own flesh?

Then verse eight reads:

Then your light shall break forth like the morning, your healing shall spring forth speedily, and your righteousness shall go before you.

I felt God was offering me a challenge. If I would extend myself to others, He would sustain me and give me the help I needed. I realized that I had a choice in the matter, and as I hesitantly began reaching out to others, there ignited in me a purpose and a sense of well-being.

When God started sending people to me (many of whom were also suffering from depression), I couldn't imagine what He was thinking! In the beginning, I could hardly believe God would do such a thing. I thought, *Surely, if God wanted to use a person to help meet mental and emotional needs, that person ought to have it all together themselves.* But as I continued to reflect on the spiritual principle found in Isaiah and how I needed to get my mind off my own needs and see others who were hurting, it all began to make sense to me.

It was interesting to discover that God often draws hurting people to those who have already suffered or are still suffering themselves. Many times, He chooses to use those who have developed an understanding and God-given compassion for their fellow travelers, which undoubtedly supersedes any other credentials.

As I realized that God was sending people my way and giving me opportunities to minister, I told Him I was willing to do what I could. In the beginning, my ministry attempts were feeble ones. I sure didn't *feel* like I was accomplishing very much for the kingdom's sake. However, I believe that ministry starts the moment we are *willing*. When we get tired enough of hurting, we will allow God to reshape us into a vessel that is willing to be used.

You can be sure that Satan fought me hard whenever I began to focus on the needs of others instead of my own. But I had grown tired of being fenced in with my own problems, and I just wanted a change. God also made me aware that if I continued being preoccupied with *my* needs, I would miss countless opportunities to minister to others who needed His touch.

I think that principle is true for all. Even when people do seem to have it altogether, they can become so absorbed with selfish pursuits that they do not have their eyes open to the opportunities that God desires to give them.

Charles G. Trumbull stated, "Christ does not want us to work for Him, He wants us to let Him do His work through us."[1] That is essentially why we must continue to give the Holy Spirit the opportunity to anoint us anew each day.

To see others, we sometimes have to be broken.

When God began to reshape my life for ministry, He first had to allow me to be broken. A lot of preparation and breaking up the soil of my heart had been going on for a considerable length of time. During that period, God had been removing things in my life that would hinder my fruitfulness. An excerpt from a daily devotional says, "Through brokenness we rid ourselves of the outer shell, the fleshly parts of us that need to be thrown off in order to bring forth the good things that are in us."[2]

As the breaking process continued, I finally came to the place where I could honestly say, "God, I really will do whatever you want me to do, no matter what it costs me personally." I don't know why we think we have a right to choose our purpose in life. The scripture says, "Do you not know…you are not your own? For you were bought at a price; therefore glorify God in your body and in your spirit, which are God's" (1 Cor. 6:19–20, NKJV).

The scripture also says in 1 Peter 2:9 (NLT), "You are a chosen people. You are a kingdom of priests, God's holy nation, His very own possession. This is so you can show others the goodness of God, for He called you out of the darkness into His wonderful light."

In the beginning, I often had to choose to obey the Word without much joy because I was still weeping with my own pain. However, as I have learned to respond to God's way, life has become an adventure; which, in turn, has energized my very soul. I thrive on the blessings that come with obedience. The rewards of pleasing Christ while helping another I can never fully express, but they have become the real motivating force and purpose that have given impetus to my life and made it worth living.

"They weep as they go to plant their seed, but they sing as they return with the harvest." (Ps. 126:6 NLT*)*

One of the first blessings and rewards of ministry came to me several years ago when I was suffering in one of the low points of the cycles that seemed to mark my depression. I was miserable and wanted desperately to relieve some of my own misery, so I began to pray for God to show me someone to whom I could reach out. After prayerful consideration, I felt impressed to make a phone call to an individual who, at that time, was on the verge of divorce. This man had left his spouse and was living in another state.

As I began to talk to him, I simply told him how much my husband and I loved him and had been praying for him to be reconciled to his wife. I told him we missed him and just wanted him to come back home. As I reached out with God's love, I really didn't know what the end result might be, or if He would receive what I had to say.

To my delight, however, I saw God answer my prayer and reunite him to his family. What a thrill it was to see God work through my feeble efforts. What a blessing it is to experience God's love flowing out from our lives to someone else. Even though I still felt unworthy to be used by God, I began to see that feelings really didn't matter because God could still shine through my weakness if I would allow Him the opportunity to do so.

Recently, I had to be encouraged once more of the need for personal ministry. One might think that someone writing a book about fruitfulness has come to the place where she no longer needs to be challenged. That's just not the case. I cannot tell you how hectic this week has been for me even as I have written this chapter. But as I read the above verse, I begin to realize that when we're weeping, it's a good time to start sowing. It's easy to get absorbed once more with our own problems and get our focus off the things in life that really matter. *Matthew Henry's Commentary* says, "Weeping must not hinder sowing."[3]

All too often, Satan aims all his guns to disable us from reaching out to others. We must not be ignorant of his devices. I have learned that I cannot determine fruitfulness by how I may feel at the time. Many times, when I felt the weakest, God allowed me to be the most fruitful.

Satan tries to negate our effectiveness through his lies and logic.

To illustrate this, I recall reading a story of a Russian believer who was almost totally paralyzed. She was confined to her little home and unable to move from her couch. She did, however, have the use of one of her hands. With that one small hand, she painstakingly translated and typed the Bible into the Russian language. She could have given up on life and felt that she had nothing to offer God or others. No one would have judged her harshly had she chosen to use her handicap as an excuse. Instead, she offered God what little she had, and God used it to bless millions.

A precious saint of God I knew personally was a little lady who, for years, had suffered with crippling arthritis to the point she could not easily leave her apartment. This lady spent hours every day praying and interceding for others. She was known all over town for the answers God gave as a result of her prayers. She unreservedly gave of herself in helping others. Bible-college students came to her with their personal and financial needs, and she would pray with them, and God would answer. God would even use her to pray for others' healings, and many were healed while she remained stricken with her own affliction.

Now I simply do not have the answer for the question many would probably like to ask. Frankly, I do not know why she was not healed. But I do know that she unselfishly gave of herself to others, and God used her mightily. She didn't grow bitter and lie down in a "poor me" corner either.

Selfless living is a prerequisite for usefulness.

God never asks us to do more than we can do, but God usually desires more from us than what we're sometimes willing to give. God is simply looking for available, willing vessels. It's so easy for us to set lofty standards of whom God might use. Remember the old cliché, "He'll use a donkey if he has to!" (See Numbers 22.)

I remember one occasion when I had really blown it. I was feeling like "America's most unlikely candidate for ministry." I had lost my temper with my husband, Jim. The fact was, I was absolutely exhausted but should have been exercising a little more self-control over such a trivial matter.

It had happened during a trying and somewhat lengthy week. I was really tired, and that is always a good setup for the devil, I might add. Anyhow, my husband and I had a little disagreement. I proceeded to have a little public fit for the whole world to see! At the time of my fit-throwing escapade, I didn't realize that a lady and her husband were watching us on the sidelines (perhaps to see who was going to win the first round!). As fate would have it, she not only noticed my little shenanigan, she also (with much discernment) said to my husband, "It seems your wife is a little upset with you, isn't she?" I was so embarrassed. I could easily have died on the spot. Since we were at a minister's convention, I knew she would probably be able to figure out that I was a minister's wife. I also realized she would probably think that at the moment, I wasn't representing my "sisterhood" very well either. So for nearly a week after that, I was feeling like the biggest failure ever, realizing that I probably hadn't amassed a lot of converts with my impressive witness.

Since I've always felt that I should assist God with His punishments, I continued with the usual penance of feeling angry and frustrated at myself. Feeling that God couldn't ever use me even if He wanted to, I decided when Sunday came I just wouldn't go to church. After all, I *felt* like such a miserable failure it was hard for me to even lift my head up, much less believe that God could use me to bless someone else. However, as church time drew near, I started feeling guilty for such childish thinking, so halfheartedly, I got myself ready.

On the way to church, I told God (again) that I was sorry for acting in such a dreadful manner, and if He could still use me, I would make myself available. I knew if He changed His mind, it would certainly be a miracle! Well, would you believe it? God, in His grace and mercy, did use me that day to make an impact on another one of his hurting children. But it was only due to my willingness to be used and His grace and mercy. I certainly hadn't been racking up too many brownie points of my own.

God's plan for our lives is to be fruit-bearing believers.

John's Gospel reiterates this truth: "Ye have not chosen me but I have chosen you, and ordained you, that ye should go and bring forth fruit, and that your fruit should remain" (John 15:16, KJV).

We will feel incapable at times because of our own weaknesses, but God reassures us that He will help us. One of the scriptures that God has used to strengthen my faith is found in Isaiah 41:14–16 (NJKV*):*

> Fear not, you worm Jacob,
> You men of Israel!
> I will help you, says the LORD
> And your Redeemer, the Holy One of Israel.
> Behold, I will make you into a new threshing sledge
>   with sharp teeth;
> You shall thresh the mountains and beat them small,
> And make the hills like chaff.
> You shall winnow them, the wind shall carry them
>   away,
> And the whirlwind shall scatter them;
> You shall rejoice in the LORD,
> And glory in the Holy One of Israel.

The scripture about the worm really fit me the day of my tantrum because I certainly did feel like a worm. But I was also a *willing worm*, and I knew that was all God said He needed to work through. Now it's not that I believe we should live our lives any way we please, but thank God, even when we fail, we can receive His forgiveness and become fruitful once more.

A lot of what we do while we're waiting for God to come through is up to us.

Joseph found that it was in the land of affliction that God made him to be fruitful. In fact, God even gave him a son named Ephraim, which refers to *double fruit*. Before I was even strong enough to venture back out into public, I began trying to minister in my own household. One day, I read the little inscription "Bloom Where You Are Planted" and began to try and look for little things around the house that I could do for someone else. One of the first things that I really felt God wanted me to do was to make my husband some cocoa cookies.

Now I must explain this story. My husband's all-time favorite cookie is a cocoa cookie that was made from an old recipe of his mother's. In all the years that we had been married at that time, I had never made them for him. God was convicting me about a lot of things, and I was beginning to realize that it wasn't just me that the world revolved around.

As I realized that ministry should begin at home, I really wondered how thoughtful a wife I had been and how much I had gone out of my way to minister to my husband's needs. Prior to my affliction, I had been wrapped up in a lot of church ministry to others, but sometimes (much to my regret), I was too worn out to notice things close to home.

God's means of motivating His children to be more fruitful is certainly beyond my ability to comprehend. In spite of hindrances and failures in our lives, God can and still does enable us to rise above our problems and begin finding a place of ministry. I firmly believe that as long as we are here on this earth, God has a purpose and plan for us.

The fire can serve the purpose of bringing to the surface the gold in our lives as a living witness of Christ's power.

We can begin to minister even when we're still suffering if we respond with a good attitude. Psalms 119:74 (KJV) says, "They that fear thee will be glad when they see me; because I have hoped in thy word." W. Glynn Evans writes, "Most of the time we have to see God in someone before we see God Himself."[4] So we might want to ask the question, "How do others see me responding to my pain or crisis?"

When we begin to allow God to flow through our lives (even when we're still hurting), others will be brought to the realization that Christ really is enough for any problem that a person might face. We then become *a living epistle that is known and read of all men* who can become a testimony of God's goodness during the bad times as well as the good times. We make a huge statement of our faith to others when we can still praise God and tell of His goodness even at the midnight hour.

This does not mean that we should ignore our desire for deliverance; it means that whether the deliverance is immediate or not, we should still choose to be fruitful. As our root system goes down deep into God's Word, we become living examples of scriptural promise.

> For he shall be like a tree planted by the waters, which spreads out its roots by the river, and will not fear when heat comes; but its leaf will be green; and will not be anxious in the year of drought, nor will cease from yielding fruit. (Jer. 17:8, NKJV)

His only requirements

All He asked of me was that I be a yielded and trusting vessel. After I had begun to recover a little physical and mental strength, God began to show me that his only requirements of me were to

- treat lightly my own plans and agendas;
- keep myself from becoming overly concerned and preoccupied with my own needs;
- be willing to be weaned from the constant reassurances upon which I had grown dependent;
- trust in God's sovereignty and endeavor to submit to His purposes;
- determine not to be deterred from the *heavenly vision* by my own self-interests and desires for comfort;
- consistently and faithfully serve God to the best of my ability and rely on His enabling;
- be diligent to seek God's guidance by prayer and study of the Word;
- believe that God uses me in spite of my weakness; and
- allow Christ to flow out from my life and give Him all the glory.

When we offer ourselves to Christ, we can become bread for others who need to know the One Who can sustain, care, and provide for their utmost needs. I realize that God leads us all individually and speaks His purpose in different ways, but I believe we must all come to the place where we are available and willing to be used. It doesn't mean that we will all be called to do the same ministry, but I do believe God will use us in some way to bring purpose to our lives and glory to His name.

While we're waiting for answers, we can have purposeful living.

If we wait until the day when our problems are over, I don't believe we will ever be fruitful. Even during times of depression, God was relentlessly at work in my life, remaking and remolding me that I might be fit for his service. I finally came to a place where I chose to believe that He was remaking me "as it seemed good to the potter to make" (Jer. 18:4, NKJV). It wasn't that I had arrived or was perfect, but I believed that He could somehow make me useful in the kingdom.

I love the scripture in Isaiah 28:28 (NIV) that reads, "Grain must be ground to make bread; so one does not go on threshing it forever." God utilizes our brokenness as a means to become fruitful. He's only interested in threshing and sifting some wheat from the chaff so that we may be palatable bread to feed others.

I believe the breaking process is necessary in order for God to release fragrance from our alabaster jar. The brokenness is not designed to defeat us; it is to make us useful vessels. It is when we are willing to be opened and shared with others that the *affliction* comes to *fruition*. In order for us to be transparent enough to share the broken parts of our lives, the brokenness comes so that there is a surrender given without restriction, and it is at this place that we will find our purpose and ministry.

There is a scripture found in Psalm 66:12 (NIV) that says, "We went through fire and through water but you brought us into a place of abundance." *Matthew Henry's Commentary* says, "As we are brought through our afflictions we are brought into a wealthy place which means we become a well-watered garden. In other words, we then are in a place of fruitfulness."[5]

It is never through any merit of our own or due to our great suffering that we become fruitful. Sadly, many have suffered but have not found purpose. But purpose and ministry can evolve *from the midst of suffering* as we allow God's love and compassion to flow through us to others.

The Breaking of the Alabaster

I had a tiny box, a precious box
Of human love—my spikenard of great price;
I kept it close within my heart of hearts
And scarce would lift the lid lest it should waste
Its perfume on the air. One day a strange
Deep sorrow came with crushing weight, and fell
Upon my costly treasure, sweet and rare

And broke the box to atoms. All my heart
Rose in dismay and sorrow at this waste,
But as I mourned, behold a miracle
Of grace Divine. My human love was changed
To Heaven's own, and poured in healing streams
On other broken hearts, while soft and clear
A voice above me whispered, "Child of Mine,
With comfort where with thou art comforted,
From this time forth, go comfort others,
And thou shalt know blest fellowship with me,
Whose broken heart of love hath healed the world.[6]

Checking Up

✓ We are chosen and called by God to bear fruit.

✓ God gives us abundant life so we can share it and be productive for the kingdom's work.

✓ Satan will always give us plenty of excuses for not being able to minister.

✓ When God sends individuals our way, He will empower us to minister effectively to their needs.

✓ Our ministry does not have to stop just because we make a mistake.

✓ Our time of waiting does not have to be without purpose.

11

COMING
THROUGH THE FIRE

When you walk through the fire,
you shall not be burned.

—Isaiah 43:2 (NKJV)

I DON'T KNOW if I will ever fully realize how God reached down through His mercy and miraculously intervened in my life. But as thankful as I am, I have to be honest; when one goes through such incredible darkness, it often leaves its scars, along with unsettling and haunting fears. The furnace life that I had experienced had left me somewhat bereft and unsure of everything. Consequently, I seemed to need a constant reassurance from God and others that everything would always be okay.

There were times when I seemed to rise above all my doubts; but then, something would trigger a memory, and my old fears would suddenly return. I was so afraid of having to relive that horrible darkness again. All I was sure of was that after so many years of struggling with depression, I didn't ever want to go back.

I had tried to safeguard my mind by reasoning that one crisis experience was all a person was really entitled to, and I sure didn't have one greedy bone in my body! Somehow, this type of unrealistic thinking enabled me to create a mind-set with a more hopeful future. I hadn't yet learned the discipline of living one day at a time, which I believe is vital to anyone trying to cope with everyday life.

One day, as I was reading the Bible, the Holy Spirit quickened to me a beautiful promise found in 2 Corinthians 1:10 (NIV). This scripture helped me to see that God wanted me to trust Him not only as my past and present deliverer, but also as my future deliverer. "He has delivered us from such a deadly peril, and he will deliver us again. On him we have set our hope that he will continue to deliver us."

I once heard someone say, "God gives us just enough light for our pathway and not a crystal ball for our future." God only promises us the faith we need to take one step at a time as we live each day. Remembering that, we will realize our need for continual dependence on Him.

God's plan for me, however, was not exactly what I expected. He wanted me to come to the realization that I should always lean upon Him and not ever rest in my confidence or strength again. Paul wrote, "We had the sentence of death in ourselves that we should not trust in ourselves, but in God..." (2 Cor. 1:9). I still (mistakenly) thought that people of great faith were those who always exuded this great self-confidence, clearly having arrived at the heights of spirituality with nothing more to prove or overcome.

Do we know what real faith is?

The truth was, I needed to learn that there are many components that make up a viable *faith*. As I continued to study many of the faith heroes, I could see that there were many of them who were called upon to endure afflictions. Their lives didn't denote people who were always on "Cloud Nine" and devoid of any trials. Many of those giants were called upon to practice a "continually-tried faith" as they walked through their furnaces of life. They refused to give up while they looked to God for His enablement.

As I looked further into the lives of the three Hebrew children (Daniel 3), I began to understand a little more about faith and its many components. Those fellows had faith *before* the furnace, *facing* the furnace, *in* the furnace, and they had faith *after* they got out of the furnace. Even though they had boldly made a declaration of faith, it still didn't keep them trial proof. Their faith, however, did sustain them in their trials and enabled them to endure. It is true that in the end, they were delivered, but I believe their faith would have remained true and strong, regardless of the outcome.

Job adopted pretty much the same attitude when he declared, "Though He slay me yet will I trust in Him" (Job 13:15, KJV). On one occasion, he boldly said, "When He hath tried me I shall come forth as gold" (23:10). To me, Job was saying that regardless of the outcome, his faith would remain active and viable.

Faith Is a Personal Thing

One of the most important lessons found in the book of Job is that *faith* must be built and internalized *personally*. When faced by others demanding that he change his attitudes and beliefs, Job firmly maintained his innocence before God and determined that he would live by the same convictions *during the trial,* which he had held *beforehand*. In 13:15, he stated, "I will defend my own ways before Him," refusing to be a hypocrite. Later (27:5, NKJV), he cried, "Till I die I will not put away my integrity from me."

> Too many make the mistake of trying to live by another's faith. Not only will it not usually bring the desired effect; it only adds to one's anxiety and confusion.

Faith to endure is as viable as faith that delivers!

In Carol Kent's book *When I Lay My Isaac Down*, she writes:

> I have found that the greatest power of faith lies not in how we think we might use it to conquer challenges we're sure a loving God would not put in our path, but in how we live—with courage, passion, and purpose—in the midst of unresolved, and sometimes immovable, obstacles.[1]

She goes on to write that God is not working toward a particular finish. His purpose is in the process itself. It is the process, not the outcome that is glorifying to God.[2]

Setting us free from the fear of the furnace!

A hunger to be set free from my fears had been first awakened in my heart as I read the book *Hinds' Feet on High Places*. One of the characters in this classic was named

Much Afraid. She (as I saw myself) was a young woman who had discovered many debilitating fears and weaknesses. I literally wept along with *Much Afraid* as I read her story and realized how easily I identified with her pain. Then I read how the Good Shepherd slowly helped her to face her fears. Oh, how my heart ached for such deliverance. Now a new and different prayer was being formed in me as I began to long for deliverance from my *fears* even more than deliverance from my *circumstances.*

I knew that God didn't want me to live with this horrible kind of debilitating fear. I had taken a lot of time observing great people of faith and how their faith remained unshaken as they dealt with seemingly impossible circumstances. They just continued to trust God, no matter what seemed to come their way. I was so envious of that kind of relationship and desperately wanted that kind of endurance in my own life.

Thank God, along with the discovery of our weaknesses, God can give us a desire and hunger for change. I wanted to mature in my walk of peace that would enable me to cope better with the difficult places in my life.

Anxiety weighs down a heart.

> All the days of the desponding and afflicted are
> made evil [by anxious thoughts and forebodings],

but he who has a glad heart has a continual feast
[regardless of circumstances].

—Proverbs 15:15 (AMP)

I was constantly anxious about life. About the time I would get victory in one area, I would suddenly become anxious about something new. The scripture refers to this type of thinking as evil forebodings. Whenever I lapsed into that mind-set, my thoughts found it easy to turn pessimistic *perceptions* into *reality*. Though I was generally developing a more positive mind-set, I would still have occasional relapses where it seemed I couldn't be anything but negative. One of the ways Satan oppressed me was with the fear that I was going to die. I'm reminded of Mary and Martha. While they were busy planning Lazarus's funeral, Jesus was planning his life!

I have asked God to make me more secure in His keeping power so that I can focus more on the present than on what might or might not happen in the future. When there are physical problems involved, that is not so easy. I do know that I am still learning the importance of being consistent in choosing to allow Christ to be Lord of my thought life.

God is still the keeper of the furnace!

> The Lord is your keeper...
> The Lord shall preserve you from all evil.

> —Psalm 121: 5–7 (NKJV)

As I take yet another look at the Hebrew children during their furnace experience, I try to imagine how they must have felt about what was happening. They certainly could have been wringing their hands, but the scriptural account mentions nothing about it. What was it that enabled them to stay so calm? Surely, their mental faculties were intact, weren't they? They weren't out of touch with reality, were they?

First of all, they certainly had to notice the fact that they were in a real furnace. Then when they realized they were no longer a *trio* but a *quartet*, it must have literally blown their minds! I can hear them talking among themselves, "Let's see one, two, three. You know, that was all there was of us originally. I wonder who is this fourth man?"

Perhaps one of them might have said, "Well, I don't know who would want to come in here to keep us company. But you know, there's something different about this man that we see walking around in here with us. I believe He must be the Son of the living God!"

Now don't you know those fellows might have gotten just a wee bit excited? I believe that as they realized that God was with them, the furnace suddenly didn't hold such a big threat after all! When we discover the presence of Christ with us in the storms of life, it does calm the anxiety in our hearts.

In Daniel 3:27, the scripture goes on to say that after passing through their furnace test, not even the smell of smoke was upon them. Sometimes, our testimonies are more about the smoke and the flame that we went through than about God's miraculous preservation throughout the whole ordeal.

God knows how to motivate us to use our faith so we will face our fears!

The Christian life is a life of faith, and there is one important truth that I believe God would have us learn: He not only wants to save us and take us to heaven, but also, He wants us to lean upon Him continually throughout our lives here on Earth. That necessitates our taking a few *refresher courses* along the journey.

There will always be limitations to human knowledge and abilities, which requires even the most knowledgeable and talented of us to lean upon God. One of the ways God encourages that process (of learning to lean on Him) is by shaking the things we have come to rely upon, which may include people, methods, and, sometimes, even our whole belief system. It is when earthly plans, circumstances, and people fail that we learn to turn to the One who never fails. We also must recognize the inability and insufficiency of *self*. I have had to learn that we are able to live meaningful and productive lives through Him and His strength alone.

One lesson God has had to teach me (*repeatedly*, unfortunately!) is that even though He will allow others to help us at times, even the godliest of people should not be our *ultimate* source of advice or counsel. I do not mean that we are to become isolationists (who need no one) or that we should never take advantage of godly counsel; however, we must realize that no human being can stand in the place of Almighty God. We must keep ourselves centered upon Him and His Word in order to prevent confusion and error.

Some things that happen in our lives just don't always have a good explanation.

There will be those times that I don't understand and can't explain what is going on, but I always have the simple choice to take God at His word and trust Him. I believe God is pleased as we strive to maintain that kind of attitude.

My sister quotes this thought to me quite often: "Our questions usually only lead to others, and our constant quest for demanding answers can sometimes be nothing more than a carnal lust!" The human mind is never fully gratified. How can it be? We are not God, so what makes us think we can understand all His workings, even if He were to take the time to explain them to us?

Getting back to brother Job, I'm reminded of when God sternly spoke to him (38:2): "Who is this who darkens counsel by words without knowledge?" Then we have this exchange in chapter 40:2, 4:

> Shall the one who contends with the Almighty correct Him?...Then Job answered the Lord, and said, Behold, I am vile; what shall I answer thee? I will lay my hand over my mouth.

When Job finally got quiet enough to hear God speak, he began to understand the contrast between himself and the Almighty. Job was contrite as he said, "I know that you can do all things, no plan of yours can be thwarted...Surely I spoke of things I did not understand, things too wonderful for me to know" (Job 42:2–3, NIV)

Isn't it interesting that Job had to lay his hand over his mouth in order to hear God speak to Him? So it is with us.

When He does finally reveal Himself to us, it demands no explanation or further questioning.

One of the biggest hang-ups that I've struggled with is that after I have searched out a matter the best I know how, it is hard for me to let it rest. My husband calls it "going on and on and on and on and on and on." Need I say more? My younger daughter once said, "Mom, you're like the Energizer Bunny. You never stop. You just go on and on and on!" I have such a lovely family.

Sometimes it means either hush up or blow up!

I recently ran across this amazing account:

> In giving a lecture on flame, a scientist once made a most interesting experiment. He wanted to show that in the center of each flame there is a hollow—a place of entire stillness around which its fire is a mere wall. To prove this, he introduced into the midst of the flame a minute and carefully shielded charge of explosive powder. The protection was then carefully removed and no explosion followed. A second time the experiment was tried, and by a slight agitation of the hand the central security was lost and an immediate explosion was the result.

Our safety, then, is only in stillness of soul. If we are affrighted and exchange the principle of faith for that of fear, or if we are rebellious and restless, we shall be hurt by the flames.[3]

So why does He allow the furnaces?

Perhaps one might ask, "Why would God allow a furnace experience?" I believe many times it has to do with His purpose and our personal spiritual growth. George Matheson, when speaking about the three Hebrew children says, "The fire did not arrest their motion; they walked in the midst of it. It was one of the streets through which they moved to their destiny."[4]

I also believe God wants to stretch us beyond our immediate faith level. He does not want us to become self-dependent or stagnant in our faith. We need Him at all times and always will. We won't ever reach the point where we are no longer in need of His help. We should thank God for that. We would make an absolute mess of our lives if we didn't focus our eyes on Jesus to see us through. If God allows furnace experiences at times, we must realize they are for our good. Now having made that statement, I'm certainly not advocating that we all demand that God bring on the furnace!

Quite candidly, I don't know why we have some of our furnace experiences, nor do I think anyone else knows all the reasons. Perhaps we bring some things upon ourselves through less than wise choices. But even when we come short of God's glory or fail altogether He still offers us His merciful restoration and forgiveness and is able to turn our evil into His good.

It never hurts to have a good soul-examination, asking God to shine His spotlight on anything that would displease Him. If we have failed, He is "faithful and just to forgive us…and to cleanse us…" (1 John 1:9, NKJV). It is important that we move on from our disappointments with ourselves (or even with others) in order not to give Satan inroads for further discouragement.

There may be those times, however, when the furnace experience may occur through no apparent fault of our own—as it was in the case of the three Hebrew children. It wasn't God who threw them in the furnace; they were standing true to Him. But God did *allow* it to happen— not only to prove the faith of His children, but also to demonstrate His power to a wicked, unbelieving king.

I have found in my own times in the furnaces that, at first, I undergo a time of great upheaval when a great struggle ensues. Hebrews 12:27 (KJV) speaks of God removing temporal things by *shaking*, in order "that those things which cannot be shaken may remain." In our trials, everything will be shaken that can be shaken.

My deliverances usually have not been quick, easy ones; rather, they have always seemed to involve a process including fear, faith, unbelief, hope, and then more struggle, where it seems all hell breaks loose (and I mean that in a literal way.) Those times are quite often an excruciating experience for any of us, to say the least. If Satan can't defeat us by the experience itself, He tries to defeat us afterward through our futile search for answers, resulting confusion and final discouragement. With relentless pursuit, he offers suggestions that will only wear us out physically, mentally, emotionally, and spiritually while whispering his lies that God no longer understands or cares.

I have come to understand that God has always been there for me and will be sufficient, even in the most difficult times of life. If I will just be still and expectantly wait for Him, that fourth man will be there in the midst of my fiery trials. His name is Jesus!

We want to be changed, but we sure don't like the refining agent who does it!

Have you ever noticed that when we are under pressure, the sweet-tempered person we've been trying to make everyone believe we are seems to erupt into a pretty mean-spirited stinker? Well, don't be discouraged, because God just wants us to see that there are a few elements within us that still need to be purified. It is during those times that we are forced to choose whether to grow angry and resentful, give up and quit, or continue to trust God.

Do I want to know Him? Yes, a thousand times yes! Do I believe that Satan wants to discourage me and destroy my faith? Yes, a thousand times yes! The very fact that I do want to know Christ enrages Satan to the point where he wants to start heating up his ovens. When we decide that we want to know God in all His fullness, the devil is going to put forth an all-out effort to stop us.

Does that mean that I have to fear that old flame starter and be defeated? No, because "greater is He that is in (me) than He that is in the world" (1 John 4:4, KJV). His grace is sufficient for me!

Will your furnace produce gold or soot?

We do have a choice in what our lives produce through our furnace experiences. We can decide, "Bless God, there will be no more furnaces in my life!" and by doing so, we can thwart God's purposes and cease to grow spiritually. There have been times when God snatched me almost instantly out of a serious situation, which no doubt would have brought injury and pain had He not intervened. But there have also been times when God seemed to let me walk through the furnace. It was in those cases that I often found an equal miracle because I knew it was His presence that made it possible for me to endure.

If I am willing to stay on the altar of submission to whatever God chooses to walk me through, He can complete His purpose in my life. I must be willing to submit so that He can finish the work that He has begun.

And when He has tried me, I shall come forth as gold.

I also know by now that there will continue to be those times when I will be required to say, "God, I don't understand what you're doing or why you're doing it, but I choose to trust you." That is the *ultimate* testing of our faith, and it is there that God is most pleased with our total reliance upon Him. A furnace test can be the spiritual dipstick that God uses to test the level of our faith.

"When the Son of man cometh, will he find faith on the earth?" (Luke 18:8, KJV)

*C*hange is a process that takes time. It is only in the fire that gold is refined and the impurities are burned out as *purification* takes place. This experience has been repeated many times in my life as the fire makes its heated demands on my will, bringing me back to a place of total surrender and trust.

I believe another reason why God permits trials is that we might learn to adopt a *lifestyle of disciplined faith and trust*. Trials serve as refresher courses to remind us that we should never get to the place where we *rely on ourselves instead of God*. That means continuing to look to Jesus, knowing that "He who began a good work within (us) will carry it on to completion until the day of Christ Jesus" (Phil. 1:6, NIV).

I have also discovered that it is easy to forget what God has already taught us in the past. We must continually allow Him to renew that spiritual hunger, which tends to diminish with the passage of time.

That is why Paul wrote:

> We also glory in tribulations, knowing that tribulation produces perseverance; and perseverance, character; and character, hope. Now hope does not disappoint, because the love of God has been poured out in our hearts by the Holy Spirit who was given to us. (Rom. 5:3–5, NKJV)

The apostle wanted us to know that the faithfulness of God will see us through all of life's twists and turns. Past and present tests victories become good ammunition for future tests, and more persistence and endurance is given than we could have had otherwise.

A furnace test is more than just a test to strengthen and purify our faith. It is a way that God shows us the *level* of our faith so that we will see the need to allow Him to strengthen and enlarge the faith that He has already placed there.

Am I willing to have a proven faith?

There is probably a fleshly desire in most of us to take credit for our victories, share our great secrets, and write a best-selling book. But Jesus is the only one who remains faithful and who can deliver.

> If we are faithless [do not believe and are untrue to Him], He remains true (faithful to His Word and His righteous character), for He cannot deny Himself. (2 Tim. 2:13 AMP)

I have often failed Him and have not always liked His plans, but I know by now I'd rather believe and trust Him than to cast my faith aside. At times, I have been tempted to give up, but I believe in my heart of hearts I can say with Simon Peter, "Lord, to whom shall (I) go? Thou alone hast the words of eternal life" (John 6:68, KJV). And I might add, only Christ has the word that can enable any of us to live purposefully.

When God began "proving" me, I was made to question what kind of personal faith I had. During my struggle with depression, I began to understand that at times, I may have served God more for His blessing than out of a desire to please Him. When the furnace of affliction first came, it seemed He had forsaken me and that His blessing had been removed as well. The only thing that kept my hope alive at all was the memory that He had been faithful before, and just perhaps, if I kept going forward, He would be faithful again.

I can testify that He *has* been faithful to come to me with a new awareness of His presence. When I thought I had absolutely taken my last step, He graciously gave me His strength and wisdom to persevere.

It's not about our great faith; it's about His great faithfulness!

We never get so mature and spiritually smart that we don't have to keep *looking unto Jesus*. He is the only thing that keeps our boat afloat! No doubt all of us have experienced the Peter syndrome of taking our eyes off Jesus and sinking. The depth of the water wasn't Peter's problem; it was his focus.

If we were able to walk on water once, it was because Jesus was there to help us. And we can't do it without His help the next time! He is the finisher, as well as the author, of our faith. Though our faith may have grown according to God's design, we can never maintain it alone.

God puts together situations whereby we must trust humbly in His faithfulness in order to overcome. When Christ becomes the object of our faith, we have a faith that cannot fail because God cannot fail. "If we are unfaithful, He remains faithful, for He cannot deny Himself" (2 Tim. 2:13 NLT). That is when we can say with the Apostle Paul, "The life I now live...I live by the faith of the Son of God..." (Gal. 2:20 NKJV). If day by day, we will depend on the faithfulness of God, He will see us through![5]

Trusting God is an adventure!

We must be willing to accept the present with all its threats, but at the same time, go on living life like it might be forever. I was very hesitant to do that because I thought I might need to leave God an escape route just in case His plans weren't the same as mine! Have you ever tried to save face for God? Ha!

Believe me, trusting God has turned into quite a challenging adventure. It is an ongoing process and does not automatically happen. At one moment, I can choose to believe and be full of faith, and the next moment, I am tempted to struggle with doubts, questions, and confusion. Sometimes I seem to reach a level of victory that I think will surely get me raptured, and then, for no apparent reason, my fears may reemerge. But when I purposefully submit my life daily to God and consciously choose to exercise my faith, I find His grace to be sufficient, and I am able to carry on.

Surrender brings peace

As I have written this final chapter, many thoughts have flooded my mind. It has been a great and daunting challenge for me to share my thoughts that (I hope) may somehow help others with their journey.

Looking back over the past few years, I have come to one definite conclusion. The only way to maintain true peace of mind is to surrender the entirety of one's life to God. One great man of faith said:

> Are you filled with doubts and questions? Would you like certainty instead of doubt? Yield yourselves to God. Are you trying to feel your way along in the dark? Would you rather see your path clearly before you? Yield yourselves to God.[6]

When we surrender our will to God to invite Him to do whatever He desires, there is that promise of joy and peace. John 15:11 says, "These things have I spoken unto you, that my joy may remain in you, and that your joy may be full." Christ was speaking this truth right after His sermon on the need for abiding in Him. I believe that *abiding fully* means that we are to be yielded vessels.

> I beseech you therefore, brethren, by the mercies of God, that you present your bodies a living sacrifice, holy, acceptable to God, which is your reasonable service. (Rom. 12:1, NKJV)

Surrendering our lives to God is the safest protection we can find!

Of course, one might do what I have done many times during previous struggles and say, "Well then, I just give up!" The only productive type of giving up is when we give up our rights and tell God we are willing to surrender to His will and plan. This is the most challenging response we can ever make. That simply means that we must once more hand back the reins of our lives and say, "God, we need your help." This involves our acknowledgement that we can't live the Christian life in our own strength, but we are willing to let Christ do it through us.

We have the choice to continue to allow ourselves to be paralyzed by fear, or we can act upon the belief that God is in complete charge. That type of surrender is what *looking unto Jesus, the author and finisher of our faith* is all about. It is not a resigned, "Oh well, what will be will be," but rather, it is complete submission to a sovereign and powerful God, believing that He is in control, regardless of what the circumstances may reflect. There is real victory through surrender.

Leave it with God.

God has given me so many promises, many of which I have shared already. Many of them have been fulfilled, and like Abraham of old, I've had to wait on others. Abraham waited many years for God to come through. He might have been tempted to look around at someone else getting a breakthrough and say, "Hey, this is not fair! God is doing something for *him* but is not doing anything for *me*."

It's kind of hard when someone else with the (seemingly) same problem as you have gets a miracle, while your agony lingers on. I've often been tempted to complain, "Sister so-and-so's furnace isn't as *hot* as mine." Have you ever done that little number?

A final look at our favorite trio

I suppose if anyone had a right to gripe, it was those three Hebrew children. (They're heating *our* furnace seven times hotter than they do for anyone else!) But God didn't let them fry because time *or temperature* really doesn't matter to Him.

We do not have to wait for a miraculous event to experience a victory!

A popular minister says:

> You might feel defeated today because it would seem that you have not as yet received the deliverance that you so desire. But we do not have to wait for an event to experience a victory! Deliverance can occur at any time at the moment I am able to "accept His timing and purpose in my life."[7]

If my one aim in life is only to be problem-free, I will undoubtedly miss divine opportunities to grow and mature. After all, wasn't "to know God" my heart's initial desire? As long as I struggle against my circumstances, I cannot allow Christ to accomplish anything in my life. I have finally had to admit that even though I didn't like what was happening, I did like the fruit God was producing in me.

It was only as I began to submit to God's plan that I found myself enabled to live out His purpose and enjoy true freedom. I discovered that I could walk in that freedom whether or not my circumstances immediately changed. Shadrach, Meshach, and Abednego acted the same way in the fire as they did when they got out of it. Isn't that the consistent way the Christian life is supposed to be lived?

Does that mean that God doesn't ever want to deliver us from our problems? I don't believe it's an *either/or* situation. It simply means that when I *must* walk through the fire, I can choose to accept God's grace and help, and He will walk through it with me. Isn't that a truth that we all desperately need in our time of crisis?

Our gracious Savior knows our limitations, and He knows how to appear just in time to encourage our faith. And in the end, we will have a new and precious testimony of His faithfulness as He sees us through the furnaces of life. There is nothing so satisfying in this world as having the sense of the "Fourth Man" who is with us throughout life's difficulties.

> For You, O God, have tested us; you have refined us,
> as silver is refined. You brought us into the net, you
> laid affliction on our backs. You have caused men

to ride over our heads; we went through fire and through water; but you brought us out to rich fulfillment. (Ps. 66:10–12, NKJV)

Have you come to the Red Sea place in your life
Where, in spite of all you can do,
There is no way out, there is no way back,
There is no other way but through?
Then wait on the Lord with a trust serene
Till the night of your fear is gone;
He will send the wind; He will heap the floods,
When He says to your soul, "Go on,"

And His hand will lead your through—
clear through—
Ere the watery walls roll down,
No foe can reach you, no wave can touch,
No mightiest sea can drown;
The tossing billows may rear their crests,
Their foam at your feet may break,
But over their bed you shall walk dry shod
In the path that your Lord will make.

In the morning watch, 'neath the lifted cloud,
You shall see but the Lord alone,
When He leads you on from the place of the sea

To a land that you have not known;
And your fears shall pass as your foes have passed,
You shall be no more afraid;
You shall sing His praise in a better place
A place that His hand has made.

—Annie Johnson Flint
(untitled poem)

Checking Up

- ✓ The Scripture plainly tells us we can expect to deal with trials in this life.
- ✓ Faith can be exhibited in more than one kind of response.
- ✓ Though our obstacles may not always be removed according to our desire, God's purpose is still being accomplished in our lives.
- ✓ Putting our lives completely in God's hands for His keeping simply requires our trust.
- ✓ Great faith is not determined by reaching a certain destination but by continuing to believe, no matter what comes into our path.
- ✓ When we can't find reasons and answers, it is time to be still.

✓ God uses our furnaces to prove that He alone is enough for the trials in this life.
✓ Furnaces are often God's proving grounds for our faith.
✓ Faith is maintained by a continual looking to Jesus.
✓ As we begin to accept God's workings in our lives, we begin to sense His victory and purpose.

Bibliography

Allen, Charles L. *The Treasury of Charles L. Allen*. Old Tappan, New Jersey: Fleming H. Revell Co, 1970.

Beggs, Mary. *Choosing to Cope*. Springfield, MO: Radiant Books/Gospel Publishing House, 1988.

Bridges, Jerry. *Trusting God Even When Life Hurts*. Colorado Springs: Navpress, 1988.

Carswell, Eddie and Mason, Babbie. *Trust His Heart*. Word Music, 1989.

Cowman, Mrs. Charles E., ed. *Streams in the Desert 1*. Grand Rapids: Zondervan, 1965.

Edman, V. Raymond. *Crisis Experiences*. Minneapolis: Dimension Books, 1970.

Evans, W. Glen. *Daily With the King*. Chicago: Moody Press, 1979.

Flower, Alice Reynolds. *Straw's Tell: And Other Twilight Chats*. Springfield MO: Gospel Publishing House, 1941.

Follette, John Wright. *Broken Bread*. Springfield MO: Gospel Publishing House, 1957.

Goodman, Karon Phillips. *You're Late Again, Lord!* Uhrichsville, Ohio: Barbour Publishing, 2002.

Henry, Matthew. *Commentary in One Volume.*

Hession, Roy. *The Way of the Cross.* Fort Washington PA: Christian Literature Crusade, 1978.

Hill, Tim. *In the Midst of It All.* My Father's Music/BMI, 1982.

Jakes, T. D. *Can You Stand to be Blessed?* Shippensburg PA: Treasure House, 1995.

_____. *Hope for Every Moment: 365 Inspirational Thoughts for Every Day of the Year.* Shippensburg PA: Destiny Image Publishers, 2004.

———. *Lay Aside the Weight.* Tulsa: Albury Publishing, 1997.

Jones, E. Stanley. *Victory through Surrender.* Nashville: Abingdon, 1980.

Kent, Carol. *When I Lay My Isaac Down.* Colorado Springs: NavPress, 2004.

Lewis, C. S. *Readings for Meditation and Reflection.* San Francisco: Harper, 1996.

Meyer, Joyce. *Starting Your Day Right.* New York: Warner Books, 2003.

Moore, Beth. *Believing God.* Nashville: Broadman & Holman, 2004.

Mote, Edward. *The Solid Rock* (song lyrics). Nashville: Word Music, 1997.

Oaks, J. B. *Rest through Praise*, privately printed, 1982.

Torrey, R. A. *How to Obtain Fullness of Power*. Springdale, PA: Whitaker House, 1982.

Wallace, Arthur. *Into Battle*. Fort Washington PA: Christian Literature Crusade.

Wiersbe, Warren W. *Turning Mountains into Molehills*. Grand Rapids: Baker Book House, 1973.

Wolfe, Lanny and Marietta. *Whatever It Takes*. Lanny Wolfe Music Company, 1975.

Zacharias, Ravi. *The Grand Weaver*. Grand Rapids: Zondervan, 2007.

Notes

Chapter 1

1. Lanny and Marietta Wolfe, *Whatever It Takes* (Lanny Wolfe Music Company, 1975).
2. John Wright Follette, *Broken Bread* (Springfield MO: Gospel Publishing House, 1957), 3.
3. Ibid., 4–5.
4. Ibid., viii.
5. _____, *Streams in the Desert 1*, ed. by Mrs. Charles E. Cowman (Grand Rapids: Zondervan, 1965), 339.

Chapter 3

1. Mary Beggs, *Choosing to Cope* (Springfield, MO: Radiant Books/Gospel Publishing House, 1988), 20.

Chapter 4

1. Charles Cowan, *Streams in the Desert 1*, ed. Mrs. Charles E. Cowan (Grand Rapids: Zondervan, 1965), 266.
2. Ibid.
3. John Wright Follette, *Broken Bread* (Springfield, MO.: Gospel Publishing House, 1957), 8.
4. Warren W. Wiersbe, *Turning Mountains into Molehills* (Grand Rapids: Baker Book House, 1973), 8.
5. Karon Phillips Goodman, *You're Late Again, Lord!* (Uhrichsville, Ohio: Barbour Publishing, 2002), 10.

Chapter 5

1. Jerry Bridges, *Trusting God Even when Life Hurts* (Colorado Springs: Navpress, 1988), 210.
2. Arthur Pierson, *Streams in the Desert 1*, ed. Mrs. Charles E. Cowan (Grand Rapids: Zondervan, 1965), 333.
3. Beth Moore, *Believing God* (Nashville: Broadman & Holman, 2004), 229.
4. Eddie Carswell and Babbie Mason, *Trust His Heart* (Word Music, 1989).
5. _____, *Streams in the Desert 1*, ed. Mrs. Charles E. Cowan (Grand Rapids: Zondervan, 1965), 333.

Chapter 6

1. C.S. Lewis. *Readings for Meditation and Reflection* (San Francisco: Harper, 1996) xiv.
2. Antoinette Wilson, *Streams in the Desert 1*, ed. Mrs. Charles E. Cowan (Grand Rapids: Zondervan), 167.

Chapter 8

1. T. D. Jakes, *Lay Aside Every Weight* (Tulsa: Albury Publishing, 1997), 56.
2. Lyrics by Edward Mote.
3. J. B. Oaks, *Rest through Praise*, (n.p., 1982), 14.
4. Tim Hill, *In the Midst of It All*, My Father's Music/BMI, 1982.
5. Arthur Wallace, *Into Battle* (Fort Washington PA: Christian Literature Crusade), 108.
6. C. G. Trumbull, *Streams in the Desert*, ed. Mrs. Charles Cowman (Grand Rapids: Zondervan, 1965), 35.
7. Oaks, 17.
8. Wallis, 102.

Chapter 9

1. Ravi Zacharias, *The Grand Weaver* (Grand Rapids: Zondervan, 2007), 127.

2. Charles L. Allen, *The Treasury of Charles L. Allen* (Old Tappan, New Jersey: Fleming H. Revell Co, 1970), 168.
3. Roy Hession, *The Way of the Cross* (Fort Washington PA: Christian Literature Crusade, 1978), 20.
4. Zacharias, 193.
5. T.D. Jakes, *Can You Stand to Be Blessed?* (Shippensburg PA: Treasure House, 1995), 46.
6. E. Stanley Jones, *Victory Through Surrender* (Nashville: Abingdon, 1980), 119.
7. T. D. Jakes, *Hope for Every Moment: 365 Inspirational Thoughts for Every Day of the Year* (Shippensburg PA: Treasure House, 2001), Day 177,
8. A. B. Simpson, *Streams in the Desert 1*, ed. Mrs Charles E. Cowan (Grand Rapids: Zondervan, 1965), 38.
9. Alice Reynolds Flower, *Straw's tell: And Other Twilight Chats* (Springfield MO: Gospel Publishing House, 1941), 66.

Chapter 10

1. V. Raymond Edman, *Crisis Experiences* (Minneapolis: Dimension Books, 1970), 27.
2. Joyce Meyer, *Starting Your Day Right* (New York: Warner Books, 2003), 123.
3. Matthew Henry's Commentary, s. v. Ps.126:6.

4. W. Glen Evans, *Daily with the King* (Chicago: Moody Press, 1979), 193.
5. Matthew Henry's Commentary, s. v. Ps. 66:12.
6. Mrs. Charles E. Cowan, ed., untitled poem, *Streams in the Desert 1*, (Grand Rapids: Zondervan, 1965), 247.

Chapter 11

1. Carol Kent, *When I Lay My Isaac Down* (Colorado Springs: NavPress, 2004), 133.
2. Ibid, 163.
3. Mrs. Charles Cowman, *Springs In the Valley* (Grand Rapids: Zondervan, 1968), 266.
4. George Matheson, *Springs in the Desert 1*, ed. Mrs. Charles Cowman](Grand Rapids: Zondervan, 1965), 151.
5. Warren W. Wiersbe, *Turning Mountains into Molehills* (Grand Rapids: Baker Book House, 1973), 50.
6. R. A. Torrey, *How to Obtain Fullness of Power* (Springdale, PA: Whitaker House, 1982), 87.
7. T. D. Jakes, *Can You Stand to Be Blessed?* (Shippensburg PA: Treasure House, 1994), 108.

CPSIA information can be obtained
at www.ICGtesting.com
Printed in the USA
FFHW010504210219
50612099-55984FF